THE LIFE OF
REV. THOMAS SCOTT LA DUE

By
JOHN LA DUE

First Fruits Press
Wilmore, Kentucky
c2016

The Life of Rev. Thomas Scott La Due By John La Due

First Fruits Press, ©2016

Previously published by the Free Methodist Publishing House, ©1898

ISBN: 9781621714897 (print) 9781621714903 (digital) 9781621714910 (kindle)

Digital version at http:http://place.asburyseminary.edu/freemethodistbooks/12/

For all other uses, contact:

First Fruits Press
B.L. Fisher Library
Asbury Theological Seminary
204 N. Lexington Ave.
Wilmore, KY 40390
http://place.asburyseminary.edu/firstfruits

La Due, John.

    The life of Rev. Thomas Scott La Due, with some of his sermon sketches and other writings / by his son Rev. John La Due ; containing also a brief memoir of his wife Martha Kendall La Due / written by his son the late Rev. William K. La Due. -- Wilmore, Kentucky : First Fruits Press, ©2016.
    vii, 352 pages: portraits; 21 cm.
    Reprint. Previously published: Chicago: Free Methodist Publishing House, © 1898.
    ISBN: 9781621714897 (paperback)

    1. La Due, Thomas Scott, 1832-1887. 2. La Due, Martha Kendall. 3. Free Methodist Church of North America--Clergy--Biography. I. Title. II. La Due, William K.

BX8491 .L3 L3 2016   287.97

Cover design by Jonathan Ramsay

asburyseminary.edu
800.2ASBURY
204 North Lexington Avenue
Wilmore, Kentucky 40390

First Fruits
THE ACADEMIC OPEN PRESS OF ASBURY SEMINARY

First Fruits Press
The Academic Open Press of Asbury Theological Seminary
204 N. Lexington Ave., Wilmore, KY 40390
859-858-2236
first.fruits@asburyseminary.edu
asbury.to/firstfruits

Your Brother
T. S. La Due

THE LIFE

...OF...

REV. THOMAS SCOTT LA DUE,

WITH SOME OF HIS

SERMON SKETCHES AND OTHER WRITINGS,

BY HIS SON

REV. JOHN LA DUE.

CONTAINING ALSO A BRIEF MEMOIR OF
HIS WIFE

MARTHA KENDALL LA DUE.

WRITTEN BY HIS SON

THE LATE REV. WILLIAM K. LA DUE.

FREE METHODIST PUBLISHING HOUSE,
CHICAGO, ILLINOIS.
1898.

To all who
rest in nothing short of
a present and full conformity
to the will of God,
and that
personal acquaintance
with Christ in the Holy Ghost,
which is the essential
element of true
religious experience
these pages are dedicated.

CONTENTS.

INTRODUCTION.

FOR nearly twenty-seven years Rev. Thomas Scott La Due was a representative minister of the Free Methodist church. General Superintendent B. T. Roberts said of him, "In the death of Brother La Due, the Free Methodist church has lost one of its ablest preachers. But few men in any denomination were his peers in the pulpit. He was clear, logical, eloquent and divinely anointed. His preaching was in a remarkable degree in demonstration of the Spirit, and in power.

"He was one of those pure, unselfish, open-hearted, sanctified men, of which the church and the world stand so greatly in need, and of which it has such a scanty supply. 'Let me die the death of the righteous, and let my last end be like his.'"

He finished his warfare about the time that the aged emperor of Germany died. When General Superintendent E. P. Hart heard of his departure, he remarked: "They are saying here, 'A ruler has gone;' but they are saying up yonder, 'A ruler has come.'"

Soon after his death, his since deceased nephew, Rev. E. H. Tenney, earnestly requested, on his own behalf and in behalf of a number of others, that a life of Mr. La Due and some of his writings be published. The matter was laid before Mr. Roberts, who advised that it be done by all means. In accordance with this request and this recommendation, the following pages have been prepared and sent forth.

In personal appearance, Mr. La Due was of rather spare build, a little more than six feet tall, erect, with very dark brown hair, dark blue eyes, at times of piercing keenness, and high, receding forehead. For a number of years he considerably resembled Abraham Lincoln, especially from a side view. Philip Philips, the well know singer, once met him on a Mississippi river steamboat, and his attention was attracted by this resemblance, which he considered very marked. Numbers of others have also noticed it, and it has been mentioned at times as one means of recognizing him in conference.

His bearing was one of quiet, unassumed and easy dignity, that naturally commanded attention and respect. In manner, he was thoughtful and rather deliberate, but not slow.

In conversation, he was instructive and most interesting; and his genial, sociable disposition attracted strangers, and endeared him to many friends.

He had good common sense, a sound judgment, and a strong mind well cultivated. Largely on account of severe application to study, his health failed several times during early manhood, and as a result he was unable to complete a college or university course; but he had quite a good education, and some acquaintance with Latin, Greek and Hebrew.

He was a careful, somewhat slow, but quite extensive reader. He made good use of what he learned by observation, conversation, reading and study. It was his custom when reading to hold a pen or pencil, with which to make marginal signs and remarks on the page, and also separate notes for sermons. He generally kept several unfinished sermons on hand for study, noting down from time to time thoughts and materials for them on slips of almost any kind of paper, and placing the slips in envelopes that had been used, and were open at one end, writing the subject of each discourse on its proper envelope. After working on a sermon in this way, sometimes for months, he would, when he believed the proper time had come, deliver it, having first arranged it, and carefully studied it again with much prayer. Concerning the objection made by some, that the studying of sermons is liable to destroy their spirituality, he said that he found it best to have the help of the Spirit, not only in preaching from a text, but also in choosing it, and in studying it. It should be remarked, however, that he sometimes took a new text after entering the church or the pulpit, and even spoke entirely extempore, if he thought the circumstances so demanded and the Lord so led him.

As a public speaker, he was of very high rank. His commanding posture, his expressive features, his very natural, appropriate gestures, the tone and modulations of his voice, and his forcible, original ideas, strong imagination and deep emotions combined to make him a natural orator; and when to these was added the unction of the Holy Ghost, his eloquence often moved congregations as a forest is shaken by a storm. There was much variety in the character of his preaching, and he said that he sometimes felt after speaking like hiding his head; but we do not remember to have heard him deliver a discourse that was not both interesting and profitable, and a few of his sermons have seemed to us unsurpassed by the utterances of any speaker to whom we ever listened. But the crowning feature of his character was his spirituality. He was known as one who lived with God.

He was a man of faith and prayer. In everything, by prayer and supplication, with thanksgiving, he made his requests known unto God. Manifest, and often remarkable answers to prayer were of frequent occurrence with him, both in things temporal and spiritual. The habit of spiritual recollection, so commended by Fletcher, he possessed in a marked degree. His mind was stayed on God. He lived in the spirit of prayer, in "the spirit of grace, and of supplication." Many will remember how he would sit in testimony meetings, and other services, with closed eyes and uplifted countenance, keeping note of all that was going on, at the same time lifting up his heart in prayer; and how he would then, at the right time, make some forcible and apt remarks, begin a suitable spiritual song, or break out in praise. His constant aim was to keep the mind of the Spirit, and in times of great trial, especially, he sounded his way through on his knees, as he said.

The charge most frequently brought against him was probably that of undue severity; but those who considered him of a harsh and bitter spirit had a very shallow acquaintance with his character. His family never saw him angry except at sin or folly, and so great were his humility and his tenderness of conscience that he would ask the forgiveness of his wife, and even of his children, when he had uttered, under vexatious and provoking circumstances, some expression that had but the appearance of unkindness. His wife knew him as a considerate and affectionate husband, whom she found reason to love with increasing strength to the last hour of his life. Some have fancied that he was too strict with his children, but his children themselves would be the last ones to approve such a notion, unless in a moment of passion or delusion. Each of them has often said that if he was in fault at all in this matter it was in being sometimes, possibly, too indulgent. Each of them was the special subject of faith and prayer, and was held up daily by him before a throne of grace. He often used the expression in his supplications, "Our children must live before thee;" and, like Abraham, he commanded his household after him, that they might inherit the promises of God. There was no one on earth for whom his children felt deeper love and respect.

He was a man of unbending fidelity to the truth. Dr. Redfield, when once asked what he thought of him, replied that he was a man whom nothing could swerve from the line of duty, and repeated with emphasis, "He'll stand. He'll stand." His powers as a public speaker might have won him the applause of thousands, but to his honor we can say that we do not know of a single instance when we have seen him, either from fear or for favor, turn aside a hair's breadth from the exact truth he believed was needed at the time. His severity was founded in fidelity, not in fanaticism—in self-sacrifice, not in self-will. His preaching was sometimes like the bursting forth of a volcano, with darkness, lightnings, thunderings and earthquake. At such times there flowed from his lips streams of holy denunciation and warning that glowed and burned like rivers of lava, causing communities to seethe with excitement, and rousing the passions of men and women, according to their various spiritual conditions, to the agonies of self-despair or the furies of rage. But we have known him before preaching such sermons to beg God to give him, if possible, some other message, and to agonize for days for the spirit of Christ, and then go to deliver the truth laid upon him, trembling with the weight of the cross and the sense of responsibility. Some of his keenest and most frequent temptations arose from the accusation that he was lacking in love and true prudence, and nothing would satisfy him in such cases but a clear sense of the divine approval. He could preach sermons that would almost overwhelm a congregation in tears and rapturous tumult, and on proper occasions he was glad to use such kinds of truth; and when he preached with severity it was not because he hated men, but because he loved them and would be true to God. The following letter shows the motives and the spirit which actuated him:

"Rochester, N. Y., Nov. 29, 1861.

"DEAR FATHER: Your most welcome letter has just reached us, and its spirit has truly struck a responsive cord in my heart, for no theme is so delightful to me as love. I think that Martha can answer 'Yes' to your inquiry, whether I 'carry this unction into all my labors.' Perhaps no one verse is more frequently on my lips than, 'For the love of Christ constraineth us.'

"When sanctified, while bathed in tears and sobbing uncontrollably, the burden of my heart and tongue was, 'Oh that everybody loved God! How can anyone help loving him? I wish that all loved him as well as, yes, and more than I do or can do.' Then I received a powerful and precious baptism of love for my neighbor, as well as for God. Some months after this I was clearly convicted for a larger degree of this precious grace, and after a few hours struggle the Spirit seized and powerfully pressed my uplifted hands and arms, while my feelings found vent in screams and laughter. Soon the suggestion came: 'This is the evidence that the blessing is virtually yours through appropriating faith,—"believe that ye receive, and ye shall have," in actual possession, as soon as you are brought in contact with your fellow-men.' And it was so. A young Congregational minister, whom we visited the afternoon of that day, was quite disconcerted by the joy which welled in crystal streams from my soul and poured forth in a holy ecstasy. Since then how sweet these words:

"' 'Tis Love! 'tis Love! thou diedst for me;
  I hear thy whisper in my heart;
  The morning breaks, the shadows flee;
  Pure, universal Love thou art.'

"God has blessed my experience and spirit in the conviction of others for the same blessing. Oh, yes,

"' 'Tis Love that drives my chariot wheels.'

"And how clearly pure love knows no compromise with wrong; for if I truly love souls I cannot bear to be other than faithful with them.

"I often warn Free Methodists against the strong temptations, which naturally beset them, to meet the opposition assailing them by a corresponding spirit. We need much of the indwelling of that Lamb, who 'when reviled, reviled not again.' Love sweetens the cross; and it detects crosses Satan would impose, for they are destitute of its gentle drawings. Satan would push and drive. Jesus always goes before and draws; and he is ever found with his crosses, which sweetly draw. Love combines the lamb and the lion, gentle as a mother and firm and bold as the dauntless warrior. It melts out self, and fills up with the pure gold of a self-sacrifice that is ready to die on the cross for salvation to perishing souls. Love sharpens the word;

for I must be pointed with my brother who is sinking into hell. My heart yearns over him, and I must, and will, be earnest and persevering in warning and winning.

"I abhor and discountenance the habit, so prevalent, of uselessly canvassing the faults of absent persons, and have resolved to propose a prayer meeting for their good, when present on such occasions; because backbiting can do no good, while the Spirit can reach them and reform, if they are in fault. I feel like pressing men to this love more than ever.

"The Lord has abundantly blessed my soul since coming to Rochester. I am sinking more fully into the will and spirit of Jesus. Souls are being sanctified, reclaimed and converted. Pray for us. May God bless your labors. I feel great need of experience and grace. I bless God that I enjoy, and am a preacher of 'thorough religion.'

"Your affectionate son,
"T. S. La Due."

Possibly the earliest recollection of one of his sons is that of the midnight breaking up of a Free Methodist camp meeting, in some northern state east of the Mississippi river, he knows not where. In the usual manner, the people were marching two abreast around the ground. At the head of the line, on one side, was Mr. Roberts, every movement and feature manifesting tireless and kindly activity, and his face and bearing expressive of the powers and joys of a leader of the Lord's hosts. At his side, in holy and triumphant exultation, marched Mr. La Due, encouraging from time to time, with look and beckoning arm, the oncoming line, his clear and powerful voice rising above the storm of melody and praise, as he led the old pilgrim war song,

> " We have sounded forth the trumpet,
> That shall never call retreat."

To the wondering child, as he looked upon the scene from where he sat in front of one of the tents, the thronged ground and the aisles of light and shade seemed as though they were some highway of the ages and might stretch away, under the leafy arches and the star-lit dome of blue, even to the avenues about the throne. There was an undefined feeling that Jacob's ladder, with its ministering spirits, rested for the time being in that hallowed place, and the unexpressed thought of his heart was, "This is none other but the house of God, and this is the gate of heaven."

Undaunted courage and triumphant faith were characteristic of the man, and though he was not without seasons of "heaviness through manifold temptations," yet he never sounded a retreat; and when he fell, it was with all the armor on, and at his post.

The following account is not intended to be exhaustive, but illustrative. In preparing it we have been largely dependent on our own recollections, and also on those of Mrs. La Due, without whose help a considerable part of the life must have remained unwritten. Notwithstanding her feeble state of health at the time, yet she repeated for our use much by word of mouth, and also, as will be seen, furnished considerable by her own hand. Mr. La Due kept, during part of his ministry, with a number of wide breaks, a diary of the briefest kind. By this we have been some assisted. We are specially indebted to Rev. C. M. Damon for the use of a large number of letters; and he and others have also furnished contributions of their own.

The sermons fall far short, we think, of giving a just idea of Mr. La Due's ability and spirit as a speaker, but will serve at least as memorials to those of his friends who have heard the original discourses in full as they came weighty with grace and fervor from his lips, and, we trust, will also be interesting and profitable to others who may read them.

The likeness which appears opposite the title-page is from a somewhat faded photograph taken in Michigan, during (or near the time of) the General conference of 1878.

Most of the matter contained in this book is now published for the first time; but some parts of the Life and a considerable portion of the Writings have appeared before, either in the *Free Methodist* or in the *Earnest Christian.*

On account of the help rendered by Mrs. La Due, as already noticed, and by Kev. W. K. La Due, the work has been to such an extent what may be called a joint one, that it has seemed best to use the plural pronoun.

May He who uses whom he will, bless these pages to the building up, in some measure, of his everlasting kingdom. "To him be glory both now and forever. Amen."

With the exception of extensive retrenchment, a few additions, and some alterations, the work stands as when first concluded, at Tyler, Spokane county, Washington, Oct. 21, 1891.

Greenville, Illinois, May 6, 1898.

Life of T. S. La Due.

CHAPTER I.

THOMAS SCOTT LA DUE was born August 7, 1832, in the town of Lawrence, Otsego county, New York. He was named Thomas Scott after the English commentator.

On his father's side he was of French lineage. Some persons named La Due, it is said, escaped from France after the revocation of the Edict of Nantes, and came to America, where, with other Huguenots who had suffered from Roman Catholic persecutions, they founded the town of New Rochelle, near New York city. T. S. La Due was probably in part a descendant of these people.

At the time of their leaving France every avenue of escape was closely guarded by men only too ready to shed the blood of fleeing Protestants, and the tradition is that at least some of the company avoided discovery by being carried aboard a vessel in barrels, from which they were released when out at sea. We trust it will not be considered out of place for us to insert here the following extract from Dr. Baird's chapter on the Huguenots, in his history of "Religion in America:"

"Next to the English Puritans and Scotch Presbyterians we must rank the exiled Huguenots, or French Reformed, as having done most to form the religious character of the United States....At length the Edict of Nantes was formally revoked....But what pen can describe the results....? Property plundered, books destroyed, children torn from their parents, faithful pastors who would not abandon their flocks broken on the wheel, the bodies of all who died unreconciled to the church thrown to the beasts, estates given up to relations who conformed to the Romish church, and protracted tortures employed to extort recantations of Protestantism! Men were even roasted in slow fires, plunged into wells, and wounded with knives and red-hot pincers. The loss of life cannot now be computed, but it has been asserted that ten thousand persons perished at the stake alone, or on the gibbet and the wheel.

"In consequence of these proceedings, it is believed that no fewer than half a million Protestants left France. It was in vain that the frontiers were guarded. Despair was more ingenious in devising means of evasion than was bigotry in its endeavors to prevent it....Those Huguenots that escaped sought refuge in all the Protestant countries of Europe, at the Cape of Good Hope, and in America...."

Mr. Baird quotes from Mr. Brancroft the experience of one fugitive: "'We quitted home by night, leaving the soldiers in their beds and abandoning the house with its furniture,' said Judith, the young wife of Pierre Manigault; 'we contrived to hide ourselves for ten days at Romans, in Dauphiny, while a search was made for us; but our faithful hostess would not betray us.' Nor could they escape to the sea-board, except by a circuitous journey through Germany and Holland, and thence to England, in the depth of winter. 'Having embarked at London, we were sadly off. The spotted fever appeared on board, and many died of the disease; among these, our aged mother. We touched at Bermuda, where the vessel was seized. Our money was all spent; with great difficulty we procured a passage in another vessel. After our arrival in Carolina, we suffered every kind of evil. In eighteen months, our eldest brother, unaccustomed to the hard labor which we were obliged to undergo, died of a fever. Since our leaving France we had experienced every sort of affliction—disease, pestilence, famine, poverty, hard labor. I have been six months without tasting bread, working like a slave; and I have passed three or four years without having it when I wanted it. And yet,' adds the excellent woman, in the spirit of grateful resignation, 'God has done great things for us in enabling us to bear up under so many trials.' " This woman's son, when the struggle for American independence arrived, "Intrusted the vast fortune he had acquired to the service of the country that had adopted his mother."

Mr. Baird says that "New Rochelle, about twenty miles above the city of New York, on the East River, or Sound, as it is more commonly called, was settled solely by Huguenots from Rochelle in France." Here, as we have stated above, the La Dues are said to have settled. Mr. Baird quotes from Dr. Miller, of Princeton, the following note about these people at New Rochelle: "When the Huguenots first settled in that neighborhood, their only place of worship was in the city of New York. They had taken lands on terms that required the utmost exertions of men, women, and children among them to render tillable. They were, therefore, in the habit of working hard till Saturday night, spending the night in trudging down on foot to the city, attending worship twice the next day, and walking home the same night to be ready for work in the morning. Amid all these hardships, they wrote to France to tell what great privileges they enjoyed."

Mr. La Due has frequently remarked that doubtless his salvation was owing, in no small measure, to the prayers of some Huguenot grandmother for her posterity.

Mr. La Due's father, Samuel Peters La Due, was very active, energetic, of strict integrity, and God-fearing. He was of quite an inventive turn of mind, and especially claimed to be the original inventor of the knotter used in twine-binding reapers throughout the world. He said that he had a successfully working model at the Whitewater machine-shops, Wisconsin, and that the secret was stolen from him. His son-in-law, Hon. C. W. Tenney, of Plymouth, Iowa, was a partner with him, and they placed models and filed a caveat at Washington in support of their claim, but their means were comparatively limited, and they failed to establish a legal right to the patent, which is said to be worth millions. Mr. Tenney, who expended some seven hundred dollars and much time on the binder matter, has said that if they had succeeded it might have proved the spiritual ruin of both families.

S. P. La Due was naturally of such a violent temper that one thing which moved him to seek

religion was the fear that in some burst of passion
he might kill some one. He was at the time of his
conversion a young man, and was working in a
carding and fulling mill, and sleeping at night in a
room where the bolts of cloth were kept. He had
been seeking God for quite awhile, when, as he lay
down one night, he felt that deliverance was near.
There was no light in the place from moon or lamp,
but he said it became so bright he could plainly
read the labels on the bales of cloth.   His burden
of trouble departed, his soul was filled with peace
and joy unspeakable; and he was given perfect
deliverance from his former bursts of passion. The
next day he drove a team in the intensely cold
weather; but the warmth of his soul diffused such a
glow through his entire being that the cutting air,
which others could scarcely face, felt to him mild
and pleasant. This revelation of God to his soul
was always kept by him in sacred remembrance.
Part of the experience he would scarcely ever tell,
even in private.

He attended a Methodist seminary for awhile at
Lima, N. Y., and was for a few years a Wesleyan
Methodist preacher in Canada. He afterwards
united with the Congregational Church, in which he
held the ministerial relation until the latter part of
his life. He was considered quite a successful

revivalist, especially in Canada. Two points in his
way of conducting revivals are worthy of mention.
One was, to appoint separate committees to light,
heat and ventilate the building in which services
were held, and to look after the other various temporal concerns of the meeting in an orderly and
thorough manner. Another was, to have persons
who came in before the opening of the service kneel
at their seats and commence praying in a low tone
of voice for themselves and others, and continue in
earnest supplication. By the time the regular service was opened the house was often filled with
strong crying and tears, and powerful conviction
was already fastened on the congregation. He was
earnest in his work, often walking twenty miles on
Sunday and preaching three times.

In the latter part of his life he was a preacher in
the Free Methodist Church. He died at Fertile,
northern Minnesota, in the year 1889, at the age of
seventy-eight, well-known, respected and at peace
with God.

The maiden name of the mother of T. S. La Due
was Sarah M. Wright. She was of New England
descent, and possessed several Puritan traits. She
was intellectual, orderly, dignified, of quite fine
appearance and very industrious. She sometimes
said that she wanted nothing about her that would

not earn its living, not even a cat. Like her husband, she feared God. Not long before the death of her son he earnestly prayed that she might be brought into a deeper experience. Shortly afterward she had a severe fall. In writing to him about it, she said that the Lord had to break her bones to bring her nearer to himself; but she expressed her thankfulness for the visitation.

She wrote us that about the time of her son's death she was one day alone in her room, when these words bore strongly on her mind:

> "Bright angels are from glory come;
> They're 'round my bed, they're in my room;
> They wait, to waft my spirit home—
> All is well."

A sacred influence filled the place where she was; and she was strongly impressed that her son, who was half the width of the continent from her, was just finishing his warfare and entering on his reward. She now waits for the summons to join her husband and children in the eternal city.

Mr. La Due was the oldest of seven children. Two are still living; John, a merchant of Fertile, northern Minnesota, and Louisa, the wife of Henry Tenney, near Plymouth, Iowa. Sarah Poindexter, a married sister, died some years since in Iowa. Mary, formerly the wife of Hon. C. W. Tenney of Plymouth, Iowa, is now in the everlasting habitations, together, doubtless, with her sister Alice, formerly the wife of John Gaylord of Nora Springs, Iowa,—both of these sisters being saved largely through the influence of their brother. Calvin, recently a Free Methodist local preacher near Fertile, Minnesota, has lately passed over into the Canaan above.

When the subject of these memoirs was about five years old, his father moved to Canada, where the family lived some seven or eight years. One of the schools he attended here was held by a man who was a dram drinker, and who had a special predilection for those branches of education which were cut from the neighboring trees or bushes. One lesson under him Mr. La Due never forgot. The teacher became impatient because his pupil was slow in learning one of the letters of the alphabet, and finally marked the letter plainly on the board, seized the pupil by the back of his coat collar and a convenient portion of his pantaloons, and lifting him up bodily bumped his head vigorously against the board, expressing the hope that it had gotten into his head at last,—which proved to be the case.

He also remembered well scenes he witnessed, or knew of, here among the Roman Catholics, especially at their funerals, which were very often disgraced by drunkenness and fighting. One characteristic incident was the following: A man was driving a team during a funeral, with his brother's body in the coffin in the conveyance, when another team tried to pass him, whereupon he put whip to the horses and racing furiously outran his rival. In explanation of the matter he said, that he was driving his brother's horses, and that no one had ever passed them while his brother was alive and he was determined they should not do it then.

One experience at this time of his life Mr. La Due ever after regretted. A charivari (shivaree) was gotten up in the neighborhood and he went. A neighbor came into the crowd with a lantern and holding it up in the lad's face said in astonishment, "Thomas La Due, is this you!" and afterward informed the parents; but when questioned by them, he stoutly denied that he had been present. Some time afterward he was convicted of his need of salvation, when this lie came before him, and he knew he must make confession. For awhile he stood at a certain spot, which he always vividly remembered, where he was just at the point of going and acknowledging his wrong to his parents; but he allowed his heart to fail, and it was not until years after that he was converted. From Canada his father returned to New York state, and from there the family moved in a few years to Wisconsin.

Before they went to the West, the principal of a seminary which the son had attended for a time became so interested in him that he wished to take him in charge and educate him for the Church of England ministry; but the father would not grant the request.

On leaving the East the father did not devote himself to the ministry so fully as he had been doing, but gave considerable attention to farming, and for awhile to the operating of a woolen mill. It is probable that this was not the wisest and most useful course he could have pursued.

The son had here some experience in hard physical labor. He, however, improved his opportunities for schooling, and while still quite young became an excellent school-teacher. His tact is shown in the following incident: A boy whom he punished complained at home, and the father came to school evidently intending to attack the teacher. He was a strong, rough man, and very angry; but he was met at the door with so much courtesy, and welcomed so warmly as a visitor, that he was quite disarmed. Before leaving, he directed that if his son did not behave the teacher was to punish him, and said that if he learned of it he himself would punish him again when he came home.

Early in life Mr. La Due gave proof of superior

ability as a public speaker. Being called on when quite young to deliver a Fourth of July oration, he attracted considerable attention. He also studied medicine a short time, dissected animals a little, and read law awhile. In this latter profession he showed so much promise that some friends of his father's told him it would be a serious mistake if his son adopted any other calling. He plead only one case, but was so successful in it that the man against whom it was decided shortly after came to him and tried to engage him for himself in another suit.

He was an earnest student, and also diligent in gaining general information. One winter he carefully read through Gibbon's Decline and Fall of the Roman Empire, in an upper room where he kept warm by staying near the stove-pipe that passed through it, taking outdoor exercise by skating.

CHAPTER II.

IN Wisconsin, when about seventeen years old, Mr. La Due attended Beloit College for a time, but his health failing, he was obliged to lay aside his severe studies. To recover his strength, he concluded to take a trip to the seaboard. On his way he visited friends in the state of New York, thence went by steamer to New York city, and from there to Boston. Here he chanced to make the acquaintance, at the hotel where he stopped, of a young man who volunteered his aid in helping him to a place on a cod-fishing vessel.

The application was successful; and he sailed to the "Banks of Newfoundland." This was in some respects a rough life, and the captain, as is usual, treated the "land-lubber" with considerable disdain; but he fell to work with such hearty good-will that he was soon promoted to a better position than he had occupied at first, and became quite an expert fisherman, making the adventure profitable as well as a means of restoring his vigor of mind and body. He won the friendship of the fishermen so thoroughly that he enjoyed the best fare they had, and was warmly pressed to teach school and make his home in a fishing community.

Returning to Boston, after a trip of three months, he was made welcome by the father of the young man who had helped him to the sea-voyage. The father was a wholesale liquor-dealer; but his family were well educated, and moved in what is called by the world good society. They owned a front pew in a leading church, and were in the habit of occupying it at least once on the Sabbath. Coming out from service one day the rum-seller turned to Mr. La Due, and said, "Don't you think our preacher is very eloquent?" He returned a rather evasive answer, but, as he said afterward, he thought, "Yes; he must be most adroitly eloquent, to have preached for as long a period as he has to this church and not hit you!"

The society into which he was introduced by this family spread many snares for his feet; and he so far threw off the influences of his father's home that he came to take considerable pleasure in an occasional glass of fine wine. With these friends he also attended several Spiritualist seances in this city, so noted for its intellectual culture, and so fruitful a breeding-place for the delusion of Spiritualism, and its younger sister, Christian Science. Notwithstanding the wonderful feats and powers attributed to the spirits, and the various means taken to convince him, he remained a stubborn unbeliever in this gospel of darkness. At one of the circles where some things were done that seemed inexplicable, a medium told him that if he would commit his will to the control of the unseen power, he would be used to perform things still more mysterious. Far as he was from being troubled with superstitious scruples, a strong conviction, he said, seized him that it was dangerous to trifle any longer with the strange affair. The mental and moral ruin of many strong-minded persons is sufficient proof that he was wise in following the conviction, and refusing to meddle any further with this fascinating cup of damnation.

He very narrowly escaped marrying into this liquor-dealer's family, where he would very likely have drifted hopelessly into the world, and quite possibly into perdition.

Some time after this, when he had become a minister, another Satanic trap was twice sprung for his feet. Twice, to his horror, he was brought unexpectedly into circumstances of temptation quite similar to those of Joseph in Potiphar's

house; but he escaped without the smell of fire
upon his garments, although one of these faithless
persons had successfully allured prominent men in
the state.   In alluding to this, and his winter in
Boston, he has remarked to us, that in several
experiences of his life he could so plainly see God's
preserving care, as to give some appearance of
truth to the impossible doctrine of absolute predes-
tination.

After recovering his strength, he entered Brown
University, Rhode Island.   He was making good
progress in his studies, and bid fair to go on and
graduate with honor, when his health again failed,
and he returned home.

He was now once more under the religious influence of his parents; and his father, especially, was
the means of arousing his conscience.   One day he
came to his son, after returning from a meeting he
and others were holding, acknowledged he had not
at times set a truly Christian example before him,
and asked his forgiveness.   This touched the son's
heart, fastened conviction on him, and directed his
mind to serious consideration of his own spiritual
condition.   It was a turning-point in his life which
he always remembered with deep feeling.   He had
attended these meetings, but they made no impression upon him until that day.   That afternoon he

went forward for prayers.   He soon professed
religion, and, uniting with the Methodist Episcopal
Church, entered the ministry, at about the age of
twenty-three years.

From September, 1855, to the following April, he
sustained the pastoral relation, with local preacher's
license, to the church in Port Washington, Wisconsin, under P. S. Bennett, presiding elder of Mil-
waukee district.   Not being pleased with what
seemed to him the aristocratic spirit and bearing of
at least that section of the denomination with which
he had united, he soon withdrew, and joined the
Congregational Church, of which his father was a
member.

In May, 1857, he accepted an invitation to the
pastorate of the first Congregational Church of
Waterloo, Iowa, and a few days after was duly
ordained and installed, with unanimous favor.   He
was at this time looked upon as a very able and spiritual minister.   When thinking of attending Andover
Seminary, Massachusetts, he was spoken of in a
letter of introduction to persons in the vicinity of
that institution, as a preacher of more than ordinary
acceptability, and greatly beloved by the brethren.

The following certificate from a church in Illinois,
is an example of the commendations given him:

"The Congregational Church of Waukegan,

"To any Church of Christ, Greeting.

"Beloved in the Lord Jesus:—

"Whereas, Divine Providence sees fit to remove from our midst our beloved Minister, the Rev. Thomas S. La Due,

"Therefore, Resolved, That we part with him with the deepest regret.

"That we esteem him as a young man of marked piety and great promise. As an eloquent, instructive and spiritual preacher, and a most faithful pastor.

"That while we deeply deplore his removal, yet we feel it our duty to submit to the indications of Divine Providence, and, therefore, We do cheerfully recommend him to any field to which he may be called to labor. Hoping that the Lord will abundantly bless him and you, we remain

"Yours in Christ.

"By vote of the Church,

"Waukegan, Oct. 14th, 1860.

"H. A. Hinchley, Clerk."

At this time of his life he held what were called successful revivals, and numbers under his labors united with the church. He was looked upon as a pattern of piety, and thought, himself, that he enjoyed a Christian experience, although ignorant of the witness of the Spirit, of a conscious new birth and of freedom from condemnation. According to the common standard he was a Christian, and a most exemplary one; but his righteousness was that of the law, and of the law as interpreted by unregenerate professors. In the pulpit he could, with his people, be melted to tears; and shortly after he could convulse his hearers with laughter by flashes of wit in a literary address before the lyceum. Like the mass of church members, he was ignorant of the righteousness of God.

In the providence of God, the writings of President Charles G. Finney now fell into his hands, and gladly walking in the light received through them he was soon converted in power. From the peculiarity of Mr. Finney's views, or his manner of expression, Mr. La Due supposed he had obtained the experience of entire sanctification. In the light he had received he walked with uncommon faithfulness for about a year and a half, when he saw that he had only been regenerated. He had been living for some time in communion with God, when, wishing to have a still deeper acquaintance with him, he renewed a solemn covenant into which he had entered before his conversion. While in this frame of mind, he realized a quiet but uncommon influence of the Spirit. Then, almost as if spoken audibly, it came to him, "You have as yet only been converted; but this that is now offered to you is entire sanctification, and it is yours if you will receive and hold it by faith." He did as the Spirit directed, and received this unspeakable gift of God, to which he was faithful until death. The following letter, addressed to Rev. C. M. Damon, Osage, Iowa, describes his experience:

"Hastings, Minn., Oct. 13, 1868.

"Dear Brother,—You will doubtless be surprised to receive this letter. I write, because—first, I think the Holy Spirit prompts me to it; second, I have become interested in you from accounts given by my father, who lives some twenty miles from Osage; third, I have lately read your letter in the *Guide to Holiness*, and I most heartily endorse the views there expressed.

"For some four years I preached without experimental religion. I was considered 'a very pious man,' and thought I was more than commonly devoted. I preached about Jesus, and read about him, and prayed in his name, but had never been introduced to him. I shall never forget the night in the little village of Rockford, Iowa, when, after a day of specific consecration, and a momentary holding on of faith to the atoning blood, for that power of the spirit which would so work in my soul as to bring me into a state in which I should have power over all inward and outward sin,—how, just upon arising from my knees before going to bed, the windows of heaven were opened, and my heart exclaimed, silently, from its depths, 'This is unearthly; this is Jesus!' Then I was introduced to him; then I knew, not merely *of* him, historically and theologically, but I *knew him* by his actual, sensible revelation to my soul. Then I understood the apostolic words, 'I am crucified with Christ: nevertheless I live; yet not I, but *Christ liveth in me.*' And when temptation came, I, realizing my impotence as never before, would grasp with the hand of faith a Saviour present, and pray, 'Lord help, or I sin;' and I found he brought me off more than conqueror.

"I was then a Congregationalist. No one understood me. I was at once stigmatized as a perfectionist. I thought I was 'sanctified wholly.' I went on for a year and a half, stumbling often, but all alone, and a year of the time in a theological seminary, where the general influence certainly tended to draw me from the Lord, although I doubt if a more pious or consistent institution of the kind exists in any church denomination. Intellectual pride was the rule—mentality, not spirituality.

"I was away from the seminary some three months, supplying a pulpit. During this time I renewed my consecration, and walked with God. I came home one evening from a prayer-meeting, filled with the ineffable communion. I went to bed, but could not sleep, God was so near. About midnight, the air was so heavy with Divinity that it seemed I could feel God. The soul was filled, and flowed over, until the body was strangely exercised. I thought, 'What does this mean?' Soon, oh! what a fullness of the love of God filled my being! and I wept, crying, '*Oh, the love of God! How can any one help loving God!*' My heart melted as wax before

the fire.   The Spirit then showed me that I had not
been wholly sanctified before; and then I made a
more thorough consecration, in the increased light,
and claimed the blessing by simple faith.   Eight
years ago last January, and since, 'All the way along
it has been Jesus.'

"I was made a John Wesley Methodist in doctrine
and experience.   God held me to preach as plainly
as he against all pride and worldliness.   The power
came.   Some fell under it.   Some found they had
only a name to live, and were saved.   Most, hardened their hearts; and I was thrust out.   I gave myself to be led of the Spirit.   He exercised me
strangely, and very unpopularly; but when persecuted, and tempted of Satan, I knew when I asked
my Father in heaven for the Spirit, in sincerity and
faith, he would not give me any scorpion of a devil
to lead me astray; and I have far more confidence
in God than fear of Satan.   I see this being led
of the Spirit has saved me from the 'popular holiness' which the adversary is spreading in this day—
in opposition to 'righteousness and *true holiness.*'
More than one, under the searching truth, who
professed holiness, have found they were not even
justified.

"I shall be greatly pleased to correspond with
you.   Direct, 'Hastings, Minnesota.'

"Your brother,

"T. S. LA DUE."

In the foregoing letter, Mr. La Due expresses his
judgment in regard to the Chicago Theological Sem-

inary which he attended for a time. In another letter, written to his father, and afterwards published in the *Earnest Christian*, he gives in detail his reasons for discontinuing his studies in this institution. Among other things he says:

"I have attended a party where some of the best students in the seminary were present, and the exercises of the evening, in which the students, and I am sorry to say myself too, engaged, were perfectly ridiculous and frivolous—such plays as whirling a plate on the floor, and if the one called on did not catch it before it fell, he or she must pay a forfeit, such as 'bowing to the prettiest, kneeling to the wittiest, and kissing the one you love best.' The kissing, if I remember rightly, was dispensed with, but the other parts were not; some kisses were thrown I think. Sublime and dignified employments for young men training to fish for immortal souls instead of wives and petty pleasure, while multitudes all around are rushing down to hell!

"Mind, I do not decry a thorough education, literary, classical and theological; but I do decry theological seminaries as now conducted. With Wesley I advocate close study and thorough mental discipline, but never at the expense of spirituality."

He was certainly right in his estimate of the general spiritual influence of the place. Even the letter of the gospel was mutilated; for the doctrine of a present salvation from sin was openly rejected, as is almost everywhere the case in such institutions. A professor one day read the seventh chapter of Romans, and closed with the remark, that any one who could read that chapter and then expect to be saved from sin in this life was a fool; thus, as is too common, shutting his eyes to the glorious deliverance of the next chapter, and representing the apostle as never rising above the experience of a man under gospel awakening.

Mr. La Due was afterwards glad to find religious institutions of learning raised up among the Free Methodists, where the Spirit of God was often manifested in power, and a present and full salvation from sin was taught and experienced.

Shortly after obtaining the experience of entire sanctification, at St. Charles, Illinois, he passed through a temptation, lasting some forty days and a considerable part of forty nights, in which his faith was tried to the utmost. After an insignificant and innocent little act the suggestion came to him that he was not sanctified. From this, one thing after another bore in upon his mind with such force that it seemed as if he would be compelled to conclude there was no such state of grace before death as he believed he had obtained. More than once he started to go to his services feeling almost certain he should have to confess to his people that he had been mistaken; but on reaching the church he would be constrained to testify more strongly than ever of Christ's power to cleanse from all unrighteousness.

In some of his struggles, alone in his study, his agony was so great that he writhed upon the floor like a worm upon burning embers, and he felt at times as though hanging over perdition and holding on only by the skin of his teeth.

One night, after retiring to rest, he believed that he saw at the back of the bed the demon who was tempting him. The lips were parted with a Satanic grin, and from the dark countenance darted such infernal malice that his flesh chilled with horror. There were no words spoken, but the language of the face was, "Why don't you yield? If I could get hold of you, I would rend you soul and body."

He looked to God for help, and peace and perfect deliverance came. This temptation returned no more, but he said that when under heavy pressure from the powers of darkness he sometimes felt the same influence, as from the presence of a powerful spiritual being filled with fiendish hatred against him.

After he had obtained the experience of entire

sanctification his eyes, for the first time, were opened to the condition of his church. Being unable one day to obtain thoughts as usual for the next Sunday, he laid the matter before the Lord in prayer. He said the Spirit soon seemed to say to him, "What do you think of the condition of your church?" and after he had stated several things in reply, it came to him, "Well, that is just what I think of them, and I want you to tell them so." Almost instantly there flashed into his mind a sermon with some thirty points concerning the unspiritual character and conduct of his people. Then he said there came to his mind a dream which had awakened him the night before—one of the only two dreams we ever remember as being considered by him of special significance. He had seen a razor partly open, the handle at an angle with the blade, and from the center of the edge oil was dripping. The dream seemed to him to be a lesson for him, and the motto of it, "Keen as a razor, and smooth as oil." The next Sunday he preached that sermon, with the greatest quietness and gentleness, he said, that he had ever known in his life; but it raised a howling storm.

One of the charges he brought against them was their unscriptural attire. The next Sunday a deacon's wife came out loaded with finery put on in derision, and made herself defiantly conspicuous. Prayer meetings were being held in which the Spirit was manifested in power. This woman encouraged a party of children at her house to hold mock services in which the meetings were burlesqued. She also circulated slanderous reports against Mr. La Due.

Not long after, as some had deeply feared would be the case, her idol child, a little girl, was taken sick and died. Her husband owned a large paper-mill, and Mr. La Due had reproved him several times for beginning his work Sabbath evening; but he paid no attention to the reproof. His mill soon after took fire and burned to the ground. These persons, after having used much effort to hinder the work of God, especially by the circulation of slander, at last fastened reproach upon themselves. The husband committed a shameful crime, and his wife by a wretched attempt to conceal it doubled the disgrace and blotted the reputation of both for life.

Demonstrations began to apppear in Mr. La Due's meetings. Some fell prostrate at their homes, and lay helpless for hours. He was much astonished at this, for he had never had much faith in outward demonstrations, thinking they were more a Methodist habit than the effects of a supernatural power. Having great confidence in President Finney's experience and judgment, he wrote to him. Mr. Finney in his reply stated that, although just recovering from sickness, and with a large amount of correspondence awaiting his attention, he was so interested in this letter that he would answer it at once. In reference to the demonstrations his exact words, as nearly as we can remember, were these:

"An experience of over forty years has convinced me that such demonstrations nearly always accompany powerful outpourings of the Holy Ghost. My advice is to let them alone. It is dangerous to court them, and awful to oppose them."

He signed himself, "Brother Finney."

Mr. La Due's position in regard to these manifestations was throughout the remainder of his life in accordance with this advice, which he became convinced was in agreement with the word of God.

CHAPTER III.

THE following account of some of Mr. La Due's experience in St. Charles is furnished by his wife:

"I first saw Mr. La Due, and heard him preach, one Sabbath afternoon in May, 1861. He was in his own pulpit, as pastor of the Congregational church at St. Charles, Illinois. He preached so exactly like a *Methodist* minister of the old type, that I said to the sister with me, 'Does that man expect a large and popular church like this to endorse such truth as that? He will not stay in it three months.'

"The official members were not long in calling a meeting and deciding that they could not pay Mr. La Due such a salary for preaching 'Redfield doctrine.' They had hired him to preach Congregational doctrine! If they wanted to hear Redfield religion, they could cross the river and attend the Redfield church, at the other end of town, free!

He replied that he was a minister of the Lord Jesus Christ, and must deliver the truth as God gave it to him. They maintained he had a *bad* spirit; they saw it in his eyes. They were sure it was Satanic power and contagious. And it was decided to request him to resign.

"As soon as he was invited to resign, as naturally as a bird flies to its nest he sought the company of those whom he had always found ready to pray, or talk of their experience in the things of God. He said he chose to live and die with a people whose theme was salvation all the day long,—always in the spirit of revival, and laboring for it.

"Days of trial came. In speaking of the letting down he went through in all the slanders of the church he had left, and its consequent effect upon his own kindred and parents for a time, he said he found it very true that he had to unlearn much of what he had for years been trying to learn. It was like coming down off from stilts to get at Jesus. He had always been looking so high.

"He attended the second camp meeting held on the St. Charles camp-ground, June, 1861, and there joined the Free Methodist Church, and the Illinois Conference, or Western Convention as it was then called. He was at once appointed to St. Charles in charge of that work.

"Most of those who were converted and sanctified under his labors continued to hear him preach; and quite a number followed him by joining the same despised people.

"It was amid these scenes that Mr. La Due took as a companion in his life work one who had known some of the toils and sorrows as well as the joys of an itinerant life—Mrs. M. F. Kendall, the widow of Rev. W. C. Kendall. As Dr. Redfield had become a very firm friend and adviser in other matters, he chose him to be present and perform the ceremony of marriage, at the house of Elijah Foote, in St. Charles, the Methodist itinerant's home for many years.

"Brother and Sister Foote were also of the band of the faithful at St. Charles. They were Methodists of the olden type, who, for their loyalty to holiness and the old cardinal doctrines of Methodism, had the honor of being read out of the church without judge or jury, and denounced as fanatics because they dared to praise God going home from prayer meeting."

Mrs. La Due thus continues the narrative:

"We passed a profitable summer at St. Charles; but in the fall of that year, 1861, Brother Roberts judged it best for us to remove to Rochester, New York, to take charge of the work in that city.

"The society there was feeble and poor, and the
work embarrassed with many difficulties; so that
from a financial point of view it looked like a
sudden transition from great plenty to actual want.
But God so helped us that we had an abundant
supply for all our needs; and of the two very things
we expected to lack—butter and meat—we had
more than we could use, so that several times we
sold to others.   Supplies sometimes came long
distances from the country, from brethren who
declared that God told them to bring us of their
substance to help on his work.   Many times our
little rented rooms, in an obscure part of the city,
resounded with the high praises of God, who thus
bountifully dealt with two such weak instruments.

"Popular as had been Mr. La Due's previous
course, it took all the grace some of the society
had to endure his close sermons and faithful, personal dealing.   Some mistook his motives; and he
seemed to them more like a rival leader than one
who had the glory of God in view.   But the Lord
gave him the hearts of really faithful, honest souls;
and they saw in the end that he had no desire to
obtain position or honor.

"Some were really converted in the midst of all
the confusion; and the work of God did not die out.

"Among the faithful souls who nobly supported

the work here, at this time, are specially to be remembered Sister Vick, the wife of the late well-known florist, and Brother and Sister Monroe. These were part of the fruits of Dr. Redfield's labors in Rochester. The following spring we moved to Buffalo, where Mr. La Due helped in the mission connected with the city work of our church.

"As the work spread, and new places were opened, it was not easy to supply the necessary help without some of the preachers being willing to be moved often, and frequently long distances, with little apparent prospect of support. To one who had been educated to look chiefly to men for his support strong faith in God was essential; and severe discipline in temporal matters was one of the means which the Lord saw fit to use to strengthen his faith.

"In the summer of 1862 Brother Roberts decided that Mr. La Due had better accept an invitation to go west, and organize a class in the south-western part of Michigan, laboring as the way might open up. When he reached there he found that those who had wished a class to be organized were a few disaffected members of another denomination, and unfit to be received into the connection. Nothing remained, therefore, but to commence from the beginning, and turn one of the first furrows of Free Methodism in Michigan.

"He had not been there long when our babe, a few months old, took sick with chills. The child was delicate; and soon the dumb ague terminated in chill-fever. Prayer was offered; but he grew worse. Mr. La Due having been gone a few days, at his work, was surprised on reaching home to find the child failing so rapidly that it looked as if nothing but death would end the struggle. Though the mother believed that she had received, some time before this, an assurance that the child should live, at this point her faith gave way.

"At last the final symptoms showed themselves, and she exclaimed, 'He is dying now!'

"But her husband seized the promise she had lost her hold upon, and instantly dropping on his knees cried, 'Martha, bring that child to me;' and as she did so he said, 'That child cannot die, so long as we obey the conditions and believe God.'

"As she sat down in a chair in front of him, he put his hands upon the babe's head, and repeated the promise which the mother believed had been given her, that the child should grow up to be a servant of the Lord. As he repeated the promise his face blanched, and shock after shock fell upon those in the room. The mother fell back in the chair strengthless, rebuked and ashamed of her unbelief.

"An aunt of the mother's who sat by, and a moment before had called attention to the fact that the child was dying, as his mouth dropped, eyes glazed and nails turned blue,—as she saw how the thrills of God's power restored the blood to its wonted channel, and the eyes to their usual brightness, so that in five minutes he was sitting up in his mother's arms and smiling, she cried out, 'Well, I have seen a real miracle to-day. If I had seen that child get up out of his coffin, I would not have been more astonished. I know now that there is faith on the earth.'

"It proved to be genuine healing. The fever did not return, nor any of the symptoms. So far as could be seen the child was entirely cured. Neighbors flocked in to see if it were really true, and went away speechless. The fact of its being done instantly, in answer to prayer, settled the point with the people that it surely was of God. From that time we had better and more attentive congregations. It seemed to be an entering wedge to the work. We often felt led to earnestly pray that God would give us, as a people, the state of Michigan in its entire length and breadth. At that time but here and there one received the truth gladly; but since then, under the faithful and arduous labors of other servants of the Lord, that prayer has been remarkably fulfilled."

CHAPTER IV.

THIS chapter, also, we give in part as furnished by Mrs. La Due. She continues as follows:

"While Mr. LaDue was yet filling appointments made by request, in Michigan, a letter came from Brother J. W. Barron, a local preacher of the M. E. Church, living not far from Elkhart, Indiana. He and his wife were old-fashioned Methodists, longing for something better than the formal preaching of the day. Living in a neighborhood where there was much zeal in politics, at that time ruled by the 'Knights of the Golden Circle,' the religion of the Bible could hardly be endured by most of his neighbors; and the Barron family were subject to much derision on account of their strict religious principles.

"We spent many happy hours at their home; and Mr. La Due was permitted to hold some meetings in Elkhart that resulted in good, although threatened

with mob violence, and once having his carriage
badly cut up. The young people, especially, were
lawless and disrespectful; but God gave the truth
such weight that the better class endorsed it so far
as to secure order and decent attention in the public
services.

"An appointment was kept up for some time in
Elkhart, Indiana, at the southern end of a circuit
over forty miles long, and at a school-house near
Keeler Center, Van Buren County, Michigan, at the
northern end. Several other places were added;
and a profitable meeting was also held at Misha-
waka, Indiana. He also attended this year the
camp meeting at St. Charles, Illinois.

"The Annual Conference, of October, 1863, at Au-
rora, Illinois, assigned Mr. La Due to the Winne-
bago circuit; and we went to our new field with
cheerful hearts. God was with us in power. Meetings held in the old hall at Freeport were attended
with the 'old-time' convictions, and the 'old-time'
conversions. We note two cases of warning.

"For a time after the conversion of Brother H——,
his wife was kept most gloriously saved, and was
often so filled with the Holy Ghost that she would
go through the aisles as if treading on air, although
a large fleshy woman. At length she was tempted
to be ashamed of this, and deliberately made up her

mind that if she went to hell she would never yield
to that joy again.   From that time she was a plague
to herself, filled with all sorts of evil fancies, and a
terror to all around her.   Her children and neighbors were in constant dread of her outbreaks of violence on the Free Methodists.   She would kneel in
her door-yard, and, tearing her hair in agony, pray
the Lord to deliver her from the torments of Free
Methodist prayers; until some who did not know
the circumstances really believed she was ill-treated,
and sympathized with her as a forsaken, persecuted
woman.   In one of her frenzies she took an ax, and
broke open Brother Joseph Travis' box of goods in
her husband's barn; and thus mutilated some of his
furniture.   At another time she crossed the street
to where she fancied her husband was stopping to
visit a Free Methodist family, and taking a heavy
clod of earth from the garden stepped on the porch
and threw it with violence through a window, intending to hit her husband.   The clod passed directly
over the head of a sister's sleeping babe, after shivering the window to fragments and barely missing
the child, to whom doubtless it would have been
certain death.

"Another case of warning God permitted, to prove
the awful danger of trifling with the Holy Spirit
when he is abroad to awaken the people.   One even-

ing Brother Travis, the district chairman, had preached a most thrilling sermon from the text, 'This year thou shalt die.' The hall in Freeport was crowded, and among the gayest of the gay floated in late, with her skates on her arm, a young woman who had delighted to attend our meetings, as she said, for the amusement they gave her when the people got blessed. She had not listened long to the sermon before it was noticed she was deeply impressed, and some thought tears came to her eyes; but when meeting closed, and it was announced there would be no more extra services for some time, on account, mainly, of a very malignant disease that was sweeping away the young people, she rallied, and with a smile said to those near her, 'That is too bad; all my fun is over for this winter.' Very early next morning we were startled by the tolling of a bell for one just her age. In a few moments we learned the sad fact that she had been attacked with the fatal disease so prevalent, and before three o'clock that morning had been ushered into eternity, shrieking and crying out in agony to the very last for help. It fell like a pall on the giddy crowd; for she was a church member in good standing, and her father a prominent minister."

In the fall of 1864, Mr. La Due was appointed by the Illinois conference to the Belvidere circuit.

Very soon after the appointment he was drafted into the army. This sudden call to leave his home, possibly never to return, was at first a severe trial. He took the matter to the Lord in prayer, and pleaded earnestly for grace to gladly accept his will, and soon, at family prayers, he gained such a victory that he could joyfully face the bitterness of separation and the prospect of possible suffering and death.

It appears that his brother Calvin generously offered to go as his substitute; but this Mr. La Due would not permit, neither was his brother strong enough in body to pass the surgeon's examination.

Mr. La Due was enrolled September 29, as a private, under Captain Thomas S. Moffatt, Company B, 12th Regiment of Illinois Infantry Volunteers. With others he was ordered south, to join Sherman's army; but they were kept lingering along from place to place, and the war closed before they reached their destination. Being away from the immediate scenes of important battles, there was considerable monotonous routine in the ordinary camp life; but he found his experience profitable, and on the whole interesting.

For about four months he served as a private; but this did not prevent him from continuing his work as a minister, and he saw some immediate fruits of

his labors. There were glorious manifestations of
the power of God in some of the prayer meetings he
conducted, and he preached quite frequently, and
labored among the men in camp, and in the hospital. Preaching in the hospital, he said, was very
impressive to him. Some were recovering, some
sinking, some expiring and others just dead. It was
a place where men were face to face with eternity,
and which called aloud to all who could yet heed to
prepare at once to meet God.

In February, 1865, as he was on board the boat
"Ariel," off Annapolis, Maryland, he was noticed by
Brigadier General Meagher, who called him up
where the officers were and appointed him on his
staff as chaplain of Provisional Division, Army of
Tennessee. The General was a Roman Catholic,
but was very friendly, calling him Father, according
to the Romish custom of addressing priests, treating
him respectfully, and freely allowing him full liberty
of conscience in all things.

At his first meal with the General and his staff,
on the steamer, the officers called on him to give a
toast in wine. He declined the wine, and gave one
with water. After dinner, dancing was proposed,
and on his refusing to join, a gay young officer
pulled him up on his feet and began whirling him
about, when the General said, very decidedly, "Gen-

tlemen, let Father La Due alone; he has a right to
his own opinions." After this, he was molested no
more, and was generally treated with much respect.

The army was a revelation of moral putrefaction.
He was especially shocked at the change here in the
outward life of some men. Persons who at home
were models of propriety, and respectable members
of society and of the church, became ringleaders in
vice. Dissipation and debauchery ran riot on every
side. He wrote to his wife at one time, "The world
seems too rotten to hold together long." The officers, especially, having more means and better
opportunities than others, plunged into all kinds of
wickedness, and threatened the first man who should
dare to report them to their families. There were
men who acted with piety and integrity; but he
found the army to a sad extent a seething pot of
corruption.

His preaching, however, was generally well received, and even blaspheming officers took kindly
his faithful reproofs. On one occasion a chaplain
objected to his preaching a present salvation from
sin, when an unsaved man replied earnestly that the
doctrine was right, and if religion would not save a
man from sin, he would like to know what it was
good for, and as for himself, he would not give a
straw for anything else.

He had considerable opportunity for reading, especially when detailed awhile as postmaster; and he was also able, in some places, to take occasional solitary rambles. Such walks were through life one of his favorite enjoyments. During them he would sometimes study his sermons, and repeat parts of them; and besides the delight he experienced in seeing the Creator in his works, he loved to spend seasons of prayer in God's own temple of nature. He afterwards said, it was a wonder he was not taken by guerrillas in some of his southern rambles, as they at times picked up persons quite near encampments. A company of several were once waylaid, of which, but for a quite disappointing providence, he believed he would have been one and probably would have lost his life.

In telling us of these walks, he has related a certain preacher's quaint way of administering a personal rebuff from the pulpit. Coming across a place in one of his rambles where a meeting was being held, he joined in the services, and finding opportunity spoke a few words. The preacher of the day was a negro; and he was not at all favorably impressed with Mr. La Due's chaplain's coat. The preacher announced for his text the words, "Jesus said unto Ananias, ye must be borned again."

The visitor gently corrected him by saying,

"Brother, it was Nicodemus, not Ananias." He repeated more emphatically, "Jesus said unto *Ananias*
Ye must be borned again."

"Now," said he, "I 'spects I'se 'bout to hurt somebody's feelins. I 'spects I'se 'bout to tromp on
somebody's toes. In fact, I spects *my foot is comin'*
squar down on dar foot. Jesus nevah wore a long-tailed
coat."

Mr. La Due had some good meetings with the
negroes; and found among them not a few devoted
souls. As the troops marched through, it was both
pleasing and very touching to witness the rapture
of the freed blacks. In one of his letters he mentioned an old patriarch who stood with lifted hands,
and cried, "Chillen, de kingdom am come," and
praised God for the long-prayed-for deliverance, as
he looked upon "De army ob de Lord." But they
alone had not suffered. The curse of slavery had
affected the whole country; and some of the whites
gave evidence of a degradation even deeper than
that of the negroes.

In February, 1865, a second son was born to Mr.
La Due, and was named by him William Kendall
after his wife's first husband. The child was a new
cord binding the father to his home; but he knew
he was in his appointed place, and committed himself gladly to the disposal of God. A relative of

his wife, a very devoted man, thought he had a presentiment that Mr. La Due would never return, and
told her not to expect his return, but to give him
up. She became quite disturbed, and wrote her
husband a letter stained with tears. He took the
matter to the Lord, as was his custom, and while
walking the street of a city on army business looked
up and asked, that if he was never to see his family
again on earth he might be given as great a victory
in regard to it as he received over entering the
army.

Suddenly it came to him, "I shall give you no
such victory."

Astonished, he asked, "Why not, Lord?"

An influence of heavenly gentleness came upon
him, melting him to tears, and then the assurance
was given, "You do not need such a victory; for I
will bring you to your family again, without a
scratch."

During most of his stay in the army he enjoyed
quite comfortable fare, especially after he was
appointed chaplain. A chaplain's pay, however, he
failed to receive, but felt amply rewarded by the
Lord in seeing his blessing on his labors, and the
salvation of some souls. The coarse food which he
had, part of the time, and the exercise and out-door
life were on the whole beneficial to him. His only

experience that was specially unpleasant was in the
city of Cincinnati, where the troops were delayed
for a few days. In a letter to his wife he describes
the kindness at first shown him here, which opened
the way for a disagreeable surprise:

"Cincinnati, Ohio, Jan. 30, 1865.
"DARLING: You would be pleased to just take a
peep at me now, even if you could not speak a
word to me.

"I last wrote to you from the steamboat Nora, on
the Ohio river, where Providence gave me a good
place. We were ordered to leave the steamer last
Friday afternoon. We marched about two miles
to the cars that were to transport us. They were
common freight cars, without any stoves. They
were packed with human freight; and a number not
able to get in were ordered to ride on the top,
where there was no protection whatever from the
cold, which was severe. Finally they rebelled and
marched for town, myself along with them, saying
that we were willing to be shot for our country, but
not to freeze to death when there was no necessity
for it. I spent the night in a railroad sitting-room,
with a large company, very comfortably. The next
morning myself and three messmates rejoined our
division, who had spent the night in a Bethel
church. We then marched to the Soldier's Home,
and there ate breakfast.

"Shortly after we performed a very wearisome
march to certain barracks, I was, while in profuse

perspiration, led into a cold room, where I had an unpleasant cooling off. I finally got a pass to go out, and was wending my way to the Soldiers' Home, a long walk off, when a gentleman and lady riding by in a carriage accosted some soldiers, asking if they would not like to go home with them, and get some warm dinner. They could not accept the invitation, when I remarked that I would like some warm dinner, as I was hungry, tired, cold and sick. The gentleman at first mistook me for an officer, and commenced some severe expressions against the conduct of officers here, which has awakened deep indignation, on account of their brutal treatment of their men. I went home with them, and informed them that I was a minister, but a private. They at once took me into their hearts, and have treated me as a son. They are Congregationalists, and among the first inhabitants of this city in wealth and influence. They have nursed me until I feel almost entirely well.

"I attended the Congregational church yesterday with them, and listened in the morning to an interesting sermon, and in the evening prayer meeting testified of what Jesus had done for me. I had a very pleasant visit this morning with Doctor Stores, the pastor, who invited me to call on him at any time.

"I wish John could see the bedstead I have slept in for two nights,—a solid mahogany, or some precious wood, with four great pillars, rather than posts, supporting a canopy of some rich crimson cloth. It makes me think of the bedstead Washington died on.

"It is quite pleasant to-day. Good bye. Jesus bless you.

"Your loving husband,

"THOMAS."

Just after the experience described in the foregoing letter, as he was on the street, a policeman came up to him suddenly, laid his hand on his shoulder, and said, "You are my prisoner."

He did not learn the reason of this unexpected arrest until he reached the station house. Here he found that he was charged with stealing two costly gold watches, and valuable jewelry, from the room in which he had slept at the house of these friends. The lady upbraided him in the most bitter terms for his base ingratitude, even reproaching him on the street in a most unladylike manner.

He could only affirm his ignorance of the whole affair. Although still unwell, he was locked up, with a notorious thief for a companion, not knowing how long he might be held a prisoner, or even whether he might not be sentenced to a long term in state prison. At last the chief of police came, and giving him one searching glance, said, "Gentlemen, that's not the man at all. That's an honest man." Inquiry and search were made, and one of the watches was found at a pawn shop, where it had been left by a young man who was waiting on a Roman Catholic servant girl employed at the house where Mr. La Due had stopped.

The young man was not found before Mr. La Due left the city, and he never learned how the matter ended.   Before he left he was closely cross-questioned by an eminent divine he had met on the previous Sabbath, and was also solemnly adjured to confess his guilt. The divine seemed well satisfied he was innocent, and also the man with whom he had stopped; but the lady blamed him to the last.

It was the only time he was ever charged with an inordinate attachment to gold watches and jewelry.

As we have mentioned, he lingered along from place to place in the South.   At last, after several months of army life, news came that Lee had surrendered.   So many false reports had been circulated, that it was not at once believed; but when the message was confirmed, and the soldiers knew by it that the war was virtually ended, their joy was beyond the expression of words.   At first there was a deep silence, as though every one was overwhelmed by the magnitude of the good tidings. Then came an outburst that broke through all ordinary modes of demonstration.   Some threw up their hats and coats, some pulled off their boots and shoes and flung them in the air, several seized a smaller companion and tossed him up, and all shouted and hurrahed until the heavens rang again.

Mr. La Due would sometimes describe the scene from the pulpit, in his powerful manner, while speaking of the effects produced upon men when they find peace with God, and exposing the inconsistency of the idea that demonstrations in connection with matters of eternal importance are proofs of fanaticism.

At the end of the war, the troops were ordered to Washington; and after a military review of vast proportions, the many miles of uniformed ranks were disbanded, and the war-wearied soldiers hastened home, glad to rejoin their friends and families and to renew the pursuits of peace.

Mr. La Due met his wife and children in July, a few miles west of Rochester, New York, where they had spent several months at the home of Mrs. La Due's uncle, Rev. Albert G. Terry, of blessed memory.

CHAPTER V.

FTER Mr. La Due's return from the army, he was given uncommon liberty in preaching. A certain minister, at quite an important appointment in the Illinois Conference, had shown considerable contempt for him, even entirely ignoring him at one time when he attended a Sabbath service held by the minister, allowing him to sit unnoticed, not far from the desk, during the entire meeting.

After the war, the same minister heard him preach a sermon at a large gathering of the pilgrims, and was so impressed and carried away that he declared it to be the most powerful discourse to which he had ever listened, and at a private house continued his laudation in such a strain that Mr. La Due, who chanced to be in an adjoining room, was forced to call out and beg him to cease. The minister referred to was brilliant and prepossessing, and might have accomplished much good; but he yielded to pride and self-importance, and the last we knew of him, according to the sad confession from his own lips, he was "physically, financially and spiritually a wreck."

In the fall of 1865, Mr. La Due was returned to the Belvidere circuit, Illinois. While here he was visited by his father and mother.

When he left the Congregational Church the wildest reports reached his father. To him, as to very many others, Free Methodists were repre- sented as indeed "the filth of the world, the off- scouring of all things." The most absurd accounts concerning Mr. La Due and his wife were circulated as sober facts. At first his father was so influenced by these stories that he wrote a letter disinheriting him, but was persuaded not to send it. Gradually he came to a better knowledge of matters, and invited his son and wife home on a visit to Rock- ford, Iowa. The parents were soon satisfied that the son had not become an apostate; and instead of finding his wife the monster she was reported to be, they almost immediately decided that she was one of the meekest and best of little women. They saw their son had been thoroughly saved, and were not long in expressing a desire for a better experience themselves. This first visit was made while Mr. La Due was on the Freeport circuit. It was the means of much spiritual good to the parents, and they became fully reconciled to their son and his wife, although still considerably prejudiced against the Free Methodists as a body.

With these prejudices, they came to Belvidere, where one of their first introductions to Free Methodist services was a General Quarterly Meeting.

The pilgrims were filled with the zeal of primitive Methodism, and came from all directions. Some twenty of them were entertained at the pastor's home, and here Father and Mother La Due had a good opportunity to observe them closely. Mother La Due sat in a far corner of the large room, watching them narrowly and somewhat alarmed. Father La Due attended every meeting, and on the Sabbath both were at the love feast and morning service. They had been watching for an outbreak of fanaticism, and now, as the Spirit was poured out, were lost in astonishment. Some shouted aloud, some leaped for joy, and many testified with glowing faces of the power of God to save. One young sister, especially, attracted Mother La Due's attention, as she went up and down the aisle lightly as a bird, her countenance beaming with divine glory, while she told her experience and exhorted. Mother La Due was convinced; she said, "That was divine." On returning to her son's house, she

exclaimed, "Oh, if it had only been my Alice, what
would I not give!   It was beautiful, simply glorious!
That was real!"   Although she had been even more
suspicious than her husband, and had been keenly
eyeing every motion, instead of being shocked or
alarmed she was convinced it was the power of God;
and the place seemed to her, she said, more like
heaven than earth.

Father La Due had argued that the requirements
of the church were too strict for young people, and
deprived them of pleasures their temperament required.   At a service in a private house, he saw a
number of them filled with "new wine" like the
"bowls of the altar," and their joy was evidently so
perfect that he acknowledged he was now satisfied
there was full provision made in the narrow way of
the cross for the young.   "The joy of the Lord"
was sufficient to meet every demand of their nature,
without resorting to any of the modern church
inventions for amusing young converts, and alluring
the unsaved.

While his parents were with him, Mr. La Due had
a peculiar experience in regard to prayer.   The
wood for the house was just burned up, and he was
unable to obtain any in the town.   At family
prayers, in the morning, he felt peculiarly impressed
to ask for just what was needed,—a load of dry

wood, and a load of green. His father was amazed, and looked upon it as presumption. But to his astonishment, before noon a team drove into the yard with one of the loads—the dry. This puzzled him; but he thought it might, after all, be only accidental. Before night, however, another team came in with the load of green wood. His skepticism gave way, and he acknowledged it was a plain answer to prayer. Both the loads had come from some distance, and at least one of them must have started before the prayer was offered.

This visit to Belvidere was a special means of grace to the parents. They sought and obtained a better experience, and finally united with the Free Methodist Church.

The family altar in Mr. La Due's home was a sacred place. He and his wife here obtained victories important beyond estimate in the effects upon their own experience, and also upon the work of God. Each one of their children was converted at the family altar, and early learned to look upon the time of these devotions as a hallowed occasion.

In Belvidere, there was an incident in connection with family prayers which served to show that the Spirit can touch the hearts of children when very young. One of the children became angry on account of being ordered to do something, and after

having yielded an unwilling and imperfect obedience, in such a way that it could not be done again
and in a better manner, declared very sullenly he
did not love his father.   Mr. La Due always insisted
on reasonable obedience, and did not suppose he was
wiser than Solomon, and could bring up his children without a rod; but he became satisfied this was
quite a serious case, and that punishment would not
remove from the child the sullenness that had taken
possession of him.   After other means had been
tried in vain, the matter was laid before the Lord in
prayer.   The child, also, finally consented to pray
for himself; and as he did so the Spirit came upon
him, and breaking down, with sobbing and crying,
he threw his arms around his father's neck, exclaim-
ing, "Oh, pa, I do love you!   I do love you!" and
then fell back into his arms laughing and shouting.
After awhile he went away into a corner of the
room by himself, and laughed in a very happy way
for a long time, his heart evidently overflowing with
heavenly joy.

One day the child was busily engaged for some
time in looking over an old Bible Dictionary, and
at last came to the mother with the book, and
pointing to a hideous cut of a hippopotamus, said
very gravely, "Ma, that's the spirit in me."   It was
while praying that the "Potiphus spirit" might be

taken out of him that he was blessed as just related.

The prayer meetings in Belvidere were often seasons of much power. Mr. La Due and his wife always attended, if not away on the circuit, and took the children, putting them to sleep on the seats and wheeling them home after the service. In this way they scarce ever lost a meeting, and were granted their desire, that their children might not hinder them in their work. Because thus accustomed to prayer and song and praise, the children would sleep as soundly in a camp meeting as anywhere else.

There was some sifting in the society before the year closed, one with whom there was trouble being a merchant on whom much spiritual labor had been bestowed for several years, at camp meetings and elsewhere, without success. Mr. La Due was pained over the man's lack of spirituality, but was at a loss how to account for it. When he would visit him and enquire as to the condition of his soul, he would make some indifferent reply, and quickly turn the conversation to another topic. One day a man bought a suit of clothes at this merchant's store, and had them laid away until he could attend to some other business and then call for them. Mr. La Due was present at the time, and after the purchaser had left saw the bundle unwrapped and the

suit just sold exchanged for another. He then let
the merchant know what he had seen, and asked
why he had done so. He replied that he had sold
the suit too cheap, and was exchanging it for
another not so expensive, but just as serviceable for
the man. Mr. La Due compared the two suits, and
found the second far inferior to the first in every
respect. He then asked the merchant if he had
done this before. He acknowledged it was a common practice with him, and defended it as honest
and necessary. Mr. La Due then told him plainly
it was theft, and must be abandoned at once. The
man refused to make any confession or amendment,
and left the church.

Another peculiar case, which as near as we recol-
lect occurred here, was the following: A brother
and sister stopping over night with a family in the
society had their rest badly disturbed by certain
well-known, diminutive creatures. They afterwards
mentioned the matter elsewhere, and the family
heard of it, upon which they asserted that not a
single one of the creatures in question had ever
been in their house, and demanded that the brother
and sister confess they had lied, or else be tried and
expelled from the church. The brother and sister
asked forgiveness for having mentioned the matter,
but said they could not deny what they had experi-

enced; so the family left the church. Many a church fuss has doubtless arisen over matters even less than this.

From Belvidere Mr. La Due went the next year to Beaver Dam, Wisconsin, where a few had asked that a minister be sent them, and were waiting to be organized into a class.

The chairman of the district was Rev. Geo. H. Fox, a man well worthy to be had in remembrance. Mr. La Due first met him at Freeport, Illinois. At that time he was a Methodist minister, and had been acting as a chaplain in the army, but was backslidden. Mr. La Due saw his condition, and in a kindly, private talk asked him to again seek the Lord. He went to the meetings, that were being held in a large hall, and when Mr. La Due gave an invitation to seekers to come to the altar made his way to the front seat and kneeled down. Before the altar work commenced, he rose up and requested the privilege of speaking. Turning, and facing the large congregation, he said that he wished to state who he was, and, as many knew him, what was his condition, and what he was there for. He then said, "My name is George H. Fox. I am a preacher of the Rock River Conference of the M. E. Church. I want you to tell everybody you see, and send word to the rest, that I am a backslidden Methodist

.preacher, forward for prayers because it is the only way I know of to be honest and get back to God, and regain what I have lost. I ask all who are clear in their souls to pray for me." He then dropped on his knees, and with a hearty and solemn earnestness called on God for himself. He was most gloriously reclaimed, and restored to his former peace and joy.

Soon after, he sought and obtained the experience of entire sanctification, abandoned his worldly plans, which had threatened to take him from the ministry, joined the Free Methodist Church, and went about holding meetings with much success. His death, some years afterward, was uncommonly victorious. As the powers of the world to come filled the room, he exclaimed, "Sanctification is no name for what I feel!" and passed to be with those who have "washed their robes, and made them white in the blood of the Lamb."

The year Mr. La Due was on the Beaver Dam circuit, he labored, together with Mr. Fox, in a protracted meeting at Berlin. One of the trophies of this meeting was Mrs. Jane S. Ray. She was a lady of talent and refinement, having moved some, we think, in society circles at Washington. She was a prominent member of the Christian Church, and a popular Bible-class leader; and had once enjoyed salvation, but was at this time backslidden in heart. She was very indignant at first about some things in the meetings, but after some bitter struggles found pardon, and at last to the horror of her friends determined to join the Free Methodists. Much abuse had been heaped upon the work, and Mr. La Due, in receiving Mrs. Ray, let her do so with an emphatic reminder of what it meant. Dragging out a rough bench, he repeated expressions that had been used about the meetings, on this wise: "If there are any who wish to join this people, this crowd, this clique, this set, this gang, they may come forward." With a fallen woman whom the Lord had cleansed on one side, and a poor washer-woman on the other, Mrs. Ray came firmly forward and cast in her lot with the despised people. When afterwards asked as to how she felt between such companions, she replied that she felt she could put her arms about them and say from her heart, "My sisters." She became a preacher of the gospel.

There was also a revival this year at Beaver Dam, where Mr. La Due lived. Mrs. La Due gives the following incident of the work there:

"One case in the class was a fearful warning to all not to trifle with the Holy Ghost. The sister was most powerfully blessed in our meetings, but having been a woman of much dignified pride, admitted the temptation that such getting blessed would ruin her influence; so she resolutely decided she would never yield to such a power again.` From that time she was silent, soon began to give way to peevish tempers in her family, and although she well knew her husband was called to preach, never would hear it spoken of again, and soon utterly discouraged him, so that he most wretchedly backslid. Not long after, an only son was literally torn to pieces on the cars, and the poor, deceived mother tried to comfort herself with the thought that it was a judgment upon them for joining the Free Methodists."

The Illinois Conference, in the fall of 1867, appointed Mr. La Due to a circuit including Hudson, Wisconsin, and Cannon Falls, Minnesota. He had visited Hudson the previous summer, and held a few meetings, and seen some good accomplished. During that visit the following incident occurred.

A meeting for holiness had for some time been held at a certain sister's house every week, and, as usual, one had been appointed on this occasion, and it was expected that he would lead it. The husband of the sister had taken offense at something, and resolved he should not lead it. So, planting himself at the yard gate, as Mr. La Due came up and inquired if that was the house where the meeting was to be held, he answered gruffly, "Yes, sir; but you

cannot hold it. I forbid you to enter my yard."
Mr. La Due replied, "Very well, just as you say;
but as the meeting was given out, I think we will
hold it;" and looking up for special help, he knelt,
and began to pray in the street. The Spirit was
given in an unusual manner, and as his clear voice
rang out over the hills quite a congregation soon
gathered around the gate, and the man became the
laughing stock of the people for causing such a
scene and advertising the meeting.

The Lord helped Mr. La Due that afternoon, as
he set up the gospel standard; and the following
Sabbath he was blessed in preaching to a full house,
among them several of the "noble women" of the
place. The man who had closed his gate against
him made a public confession, and stepping forward
to the desk meekly asked if he might join the class.
From that time the work continued to move on with
success, in the ordinary means of grace.

An experience Mr. La Due had at Hudson, is thus
related by his wife:

"During the meetings held in the chapel, a merchant's wife, who was not friendly to one of the
Free Methodist sisters, was one evening amusing
herself, during prayer, with the sister's earnest gestures, when Mr. La Due, attracted by the noise,
looked up suddenly and spied the play. Rising

from his knees, he felt it to be his duty to rebuke such conduct, as it had already attracted attention and made disturbance. The woman at once moved abruptly to the end of the seat, and denied having had any part whatever in the matter. Mr. La Due replied, that he wished to be pardoned if he had made such a blunder, but that he was not yet convinced he had.

"The woman left in a rage, and next morning, as the family were sitting down to breakfast, a police officer knocked at the door, and read his order for an arrest. He was asked to wait a few moments until the family had their morning prayers; but he insisted that the prisoner should go with him at once, and Mr. La Due calmly prepared to follow. The children were filled with alarm, and family prayer, which was conducted by the mother, was a time of earnest supplication. Procuring some one to stay with the children a few hours, the mother went with some of the sisters to the court-room, where most of the society were met.

"The chief of police was in high spirits over the fine opportunity thus afforded him of ridiculing and abusing the people he so detested. The prosecuting attorney was more than his equal. No common words would express his thoughts. Low cant, and blasphemy of the most shocking kind followed in

quick succession, until the truly pious present began
to fear the man would be struck to the floor a
corpse. The police justice, before whom the prisoner was tried, refused him a chance to speak until
after he had been sentenced to a fine, when the lawyer who had volunteered for the defence obtained
permission for him to say a few words. In a calm
and candid manner Mr. La Due plainly stated the
facts, and upset all the arguments that had been
used, until every lawyer present looked amazed.

"The effect on the crowded house was electric.
An old infidel, a miser, took the floor, and after a
speech of some force said, as he took his hat, put a
dollar into it, and began moving around the room,
'Gentlemen, this man is not going to jail; we will
pay his fine. The twenty-five dollars shall come out
of some other pockets than his.' The miser carried
the day, and after he had raised the fine remarked,
in reference to Mr. La Due's conduct and spirit,
'That comes the nearest to what you call the religion of the Bible of anything I ever saw. If there *is*
truth in it, that is the real thing.'

"That night an 'Indignation Meeting' was held in
one of the principal stores of the place, and the
merchant rallied the lawyers, and others of the opposing party, who came in to see the result of the
meeting. 'Boys,' said he, 'you have done an excel-

lent thing for these Free Methodists. You thought
to hold them up to contempt, whereas you have put
yourselves to considerable trouble, and while they
in their quiet way resorted to prayer, you have low-
ered yourselves by an attempt to blacken them, and
the devil has had to foot the bill.' He concluded
by saying, 'You have made them ten friends where
they had one, and their congregations will be
doubled.'

"This was literally true. The little chapel was
filled to overflowing the following Sabbath; and the
mayor himself came in the evening and volunteered
his services, saying to Mr. La Due, 'I will see that
you are not molested again, and will come myself,
or send a man to see that my order is carried out.
I am ashamed that such an outrage as your trial has
ever happened here.' When the circuit judge, the
husband of a member of the Free Methodist society,
returned home a few days after, he tried to get the
lawyers to tell how they went to work to prove that
Mr. La Due had 'disturbed the public peace of a
private individual.' He declared it was the first case
of the kind on record. This, together with the ridicule of their work by the St. Paul papers, turned the
tide of opposition, so that there was no need of further defense.

"The Lord took care of his own cause. Public

sentiment became so strong against the woman who had arrested Mr. La Due, and against her husband, that the latter sold out as soon as he could and moved away. The attorney who had so wickedly and blasphemously ridiculed God's people before the crowd in the court-room never pleaded another case. A few days after, he was stricken down with some disease of such a nature that no one was allowed to see the poor man, except his intimate friends, and a minister at the last. The general verdict in the place was, 'A judgment from God.' 'Great fear fell on all the people.' The large court-house was offered us, and for some time it was filled at the preaching services.

"Mr. La Due counted this one of his best years, and the trial as a rich experience. There were very pleasant associations formed here, that were lasting. It was also the birth-place of his only daughter."

CHAPTER VI.

T the Illinois conference of September, 1868, Mr. La Due was appointed chairman of the Minnesota District. He made his home at first in Hastings, a city on the Mississippi river, just above the mouth of the St. Croix. The following account of two who were benefited by his labors in this place is by his wife:

"Our way into Hastings was opened in a very marked manner. We were passing the town on a very cold day in December, when we felt as if we would be obliged to stop and ask the privilege of warming awhile at a private house. As Mr. La Due had entered the house to ask this privilege, a lady who was at work in the room looked up in wonder at seeing a preacher, and enquired if we were traveling far. On his answering her that we were on the Lord's business, and looking up his sheep, the tears came into her eyes, and she said in reply that no one had been there on that errand for many, many a day. Mr. La Due began to praise God, as he saw the tenderness of heart manifested, and her tears flowed faster; and she soon after exclaimed, 'I did not know as I ever should hear God praised again. I am favored this day indeed!' She hastened to prepare us a warm meal, and we were refreshed for the rest of our journey as we little expected.

"A little conversation revealed that we had providentially been led to call upon a family in deep trouble. They had been first in all the work and honors of the M. E. church, when very suddenly one of the family had been decoyed into a well-instructed club of business men who made it their habit to lie in wait for married men, and by some means drain their purses. This time they had made a tool of a young man who, though sharp, was too young yet in scheming to escape detection as a forger, and had been imprisoned for a long term. This chilled all the church friendship the family had known, and they were dropped from the circle of respectable friends; even by class-leader, preacher and all, and left to the cold mercies of a cruel, heartless world. God only knew the sorrow of that mother's heart. The season of prayer we enjoyed that day will never be forgotten.

"We had the pleasure of seeing the heads of that family truly saved and welcomed to the church, and

of knowing that the son was finally delivered from
at least worldly ruin. This poor, sorrowing mother
had her tears wiped away, and her face shone with
heavenly radiance. She proved an angel of mercy
to us in many a dark hour after that, in temporal
things; and we proved by a close acquaintance that
she was one of those noblest works of God—a woman
who was always relieving our wants without our
mentioning them, and often helping the needy without letting it be known, if possible, from where the
help came."

Mr. La Due labored this year chiefly in Cherry
Valley,—a country district near Cannon Falls,—and
at Pine Island, and also occasionally at various other
points in that region of the state.

The following letter was written to Rev. C. M.
Damon, who was then a Methodist minister living
in Iowa, and of whom we shall have more to say
a little farther on:

"Hastings, Minn., Nov. 6, 1868.

"Dear Brother Damon: Your welcome letter is
received. We are rejoiced at your evident sympathy with Jesus, and that we can salute another
brother in the Lord, in these days of heartless formalism.

"Your apprehensions concerning the deplorable
condition of the great mass of church members are
doubtless too true. Never did Satan so chuckle over

the grand deception he is now practicing in the shape
of what is termed orthodox religion; never were so
many feeding on ashes, a deceived heart having
turned them aside, and going down to the grave
with a lie in their right hand, not knowing it—confirmed in their delusion by daubers with untempered
mortar, false prophets crying, Peace, when there is
no peace, physicians guilty of the most horrible
malpractice in healing the hurt of the daughter of
God's people slightly.

"The church in Christ's day was most terribly
mistaken as to its moral condition. But the church
now is in more fearful error; for the Jews boasted of
acknowledging God, while they of this day boast, in
spirit at least, of acknowledging both God the Father
and Jesus Christ, while they dishonor the one by open
and constant violation of his law, and make a mere
convenient thing of the other,—a pack-horse to carry
off the load of the guilt of their sins, while they sin
every day, confess they do, and manifestly intend to
continue to do so, having no real compunction or
penitence, and yet at the end they will throw all on
Jesus, and manage to get into heaven. Oh! God-
insulting, Christ-dishonoring generation; worldlings
to all intents, dressed in the livery of church forms,
and connections, and professions— clear below the
ancient Pharisee; willing that Jesus should be Priest
to atone, but they King, instead of him, to dictate
and rule their conduct. Verily, these are perilous
times; and the wonder is that I, or you, or any are
truly saved.

"I think you are sanctified wholly. I understand your temptations to irritability. The influences of Satan are very similar to the motions of the carnal heart. For instance: Satan can tempt the pure heart to impatience. How do we know such a temptation, but from a feeling like impatience thrown by Satan around the heart, wholly from him, and yet seeming very much to belong to the heart itself? The Lord revealed this to me after some months of trial of my faith in this direction.

"I found myself lacking in power and freedom after my sanctification. I besought power. The Spirit came, exercising me strangely, in a way very 'foolish' to 'the natural man'—such simple, child-like laughter, sometimes jumpings, and even dancings for joy, like David 'before the Lord.' But I had sincerely asked my Father for the Spirit. I believed I should receive it, and nothing else. I obtained all the benefits of the baptism in a way which kept me from being puffed up over it.

"Many stop at entire sanctification, unwilling to be led by the Spirit, and lapse into the popular holiness which Satan is propagating.

"I see no sweeping revivals as yet under my labors; but precious souls are saved, and some of them very marked cases, especially some of the choice members of other churches.

"Great persecution. Last winter I was arrested by a clique of Masons, and fined twenty-five dollars for disturbing the public peace; but, oh, how Jesus helped me triumph, and turned the town in our favor! We go forth trusting God for a support, no matter whether any class or church exists in that locality. And we have all and abound. Trying conflicts with the arch-fiend, and triumphs through Jesus. I wish you could visit us at Hastings, and spend some weeks with us. The idea of going to Evanston impresses me unfavorably. God held me to giving up a theological seminary.

"I commenced this some time ago, but have been prevented from sending it. I will try to answer more promptly.

"Your Bro. in the Lord,

"T. S. La Due."

Mr. La Due's work at this time, as during much of his ministry, was opening up and putting in shape new fields. This subjected him and his family to the trials unavoidably connected with such labors. It being sometimes necessary to live around among the people for weeks, and even months, his children were thrown into peculiar temptations from the various circumstances and associations in which they were placed; and there were occasions when from this cause, as well as others, all the wisdom and grace of the parents were severely tested. The prospect for temporal support was also often such as would utterly dishearten any one not wholly devoted to God, and willing to trust him in any place he might appoint. But he found the work, on the whole, unspeakably delightful, because of the blessing of the Lord. When asked once where he would prefer to be appointed, he said, "Send me out on the frontier." He went into such fields joyfully; and he was cared for temporally, and saw the salvation of souls.

The Minnesota and Northern Iowa conference was raised up chiefly by his labors this year and afterward, and from that conference the work has since spread out on every side.

The preacher who began the regular work of organized Free Methodism in Minnesota was Rev. Geo. H. Fox, and when Mr. La Due came to the state a few had been received into the connection. In Father Sumner's house in Cherry Valley, Goodhue County, was the beginning of a pilgrim church which may well be said to have been the parent class of the Minnesota and North Iowa Conference.

The prayer meetings, quarterly services, and grove meetings which Mr. La Due held in Cherry Valley in the years 1867 and 1868, were often marked occasions; but in the early part of 1869 there was a revival of uncommon power.

After the meeting had been going on about a week, a young woman became so burdened one night for one of her brothers that she went to the back part of the school-house, and falling on her knees poured out her soul in an agony of prayer. The brother and a companion who was sitting with him were so wrought upon that they leaped over her, as she kneeled at the end of the seat in the aisle, and rushed for the door. One of them started running for home. He afterward said that hell seemed just before him, and that at every step he was literally in danger of plunging into it. He had gone but a short distance when he turned again, and joining his companion they both entered the school-house, and without any invitation made their way to the altar and began crying for mercy.

They did not obtain relief that night. The next morning the young woman's brother came to his father, and said that he had a confession to make. He then told that he, with several other young men, had sometimes taken horses secretly, at night, and ridden about the country, and in one of these frolics had stolen a quantity of honey from a neighbor's stand of bees. He felt that he ought to go and make the wrong right. His father was much moved, and gladly told him to go and do as he had said. It was a heavy cross; but he went and settled the matter, and on the way found peace with God, and such a blessing that he could hardly keep on the horse he was riding.

The other young man had been a ringleader of those who made sport of the meetings, even going so far as to preach a mock sermon. After some straightening up, very similar to what his companion had been held to, he was converted one night with a storm of demonstration beyond anything he had attempted to imitate, shaking a wood box down on which he was sitting, and then leaping up and shouting, "Hurrah for Jesus!"

From the starting of these two, the work went on in power, and numbers were saved.

One of Mr. Sumner's sons was a professor of religion at this time, and had been assisting in a Methodist revival, together with his wife; but he saw he was backslidden, made a public confession, and sought the Lord again until he found him. Going home one day he told his wife he intended to join the Free Methodist class. She replied that if he did, he might go home to his father's, and she would go to hers. She then urged him to put it off for a month, or at least a week. He answered no, he should join that night. While he was gone that evening she was brought under conviction, and found that she, too, had only a profession and needed to be converted. One of the points of separation she had to make was in regard to dress. Her husband, during the war, had sent her from the army a fine cloak loaded with beads. She was convicted that she must take them off. Small as such a matter seemed, it was for some time more than her proud heart could endure. At last, however, she took the cloak and performed the heavy task. As the last bead was removed it seemed as though a mountain was rolled off from her heart, the glory of God came down, and when her husband returned he found her leaping and praising God. She afterward held up her husband's hands while he did the work of a Free Methodist preacher.

People attended this meeting from all parts of the surrounding neighborhood, some coming quite a distance; and the valley often rang with the songs and praises of those on their way to and from the services.

During the summer seasons meetings were held in groves, and at various school-houses, and large loads would come, from long distances at times, singing and praising God as they drove through the country, spreading conviction and a gracious influence for good far and wide.

Persons blessed in the work of God in this region have since carried the results of the benefits there received hundreds and even thousands of miles in various directions. Some are still living, and walking by the same rule; and some have made most fearful shipwreck of the faith.

Two, especially, we remember as striking ex-

amples of those whose latter end becomes worse
than their beginning.   One was a man who was
blessed in this revival, and who for a time warmly
supported Mr. La Due; but after awhile he let in a
feeling of enmity against several persons, drifted
away into fanaticism, and finally became one of Mr.
La Due's most bitter opposers.   In a meeting one
evening this man went up and down the house
shouting, in a frenzy of defiance, "Glory to God!"
and encouraging some who opposed the meeting by
crying out, "Hold on; we shall have the victory!"
The spirit of opposition and confusion seemed for a
time to have control of everything, and all Mr.
La Due could do was to look up to God and pray
that he would take the affair into his own hands.
Soon he heard the young sister already alluded to
saying, almost in a whisper, "The *everlasting* glory.
The *everlasting* glory."   And as she repeated it in a
louder and louder tone of voice the Holy Ghost
came, the man who was shouting "Glory" stopped
as though choked, and backing Mr. La Due up
against a door shook his fist at him, fully revealing
to every one the spirit that possessed him, and thus
breaking much of the strength of the opposition.

Another person became unwilling to continue
bearing the cross, and fell a prey to the grossest
deiusion. The Mormons came into the neighbor-

hood, and this young man accepted their teaching, was baptized, and consecrated by the laying on of hands. He declared that when the elder's hands were laid on his head he felt the power of God go through his body from his head to his feet. It is certain there was a great change in him, for his very countenance was altered from that time and his actions were anything but holy.

To illustrate the bitterness of the opposition above mentioned, one more incident may suffice. The opposers were helped for a time by an elderly Methodist local preacher, who called the Free Methodists "the scum of the swill barrel."

Soon after the revival spoken of in the present chapter Mr. La Due fell sick. The disease took the form of what was thought to be a typhoid deposit, causing one of his knees to swell to about the size of a peck measure, and was accompanied with chills and fever and such exquisite pains that although a man of uncommon fortitude and much endurance he sometimes wept like a child. He was also much burdened for the work. Some rejoiced that he was confined, and predicted he would not recover. The work, however, went on, and some were saved during his illness. After his patience and grace had been tried for several weeks, he obtained a victory one morning over suffering, and shouted aloud, giving glory to God and saying Amen to his will. In half an hour the swelling broke; and he was soon able to be carried to meetings and preach sitting in a chair, while some who had rejoiced at the prospect of his death looked upon him, as he passed by praising God, with almost as much astonishment as if he had come back from the grave. It was thought that the swelling possibly saved him from a fatal run of fever, and it was certainly a means of grace.

In April of this year his goods were moved from Hastings to Cherry Valley, where the family remained until the following year.

About this time the Mormons made some trouble in that neighborhood. Several of them, coming in at various times, zealously spread their views; and although at least one of them was doubtless grossly licentious they succeeded in making some converts, among them a young man already mentioned. They troubled the Free Methodist meetings for a time, but were so frightened at last, in a certain service, that they afterward seemed to think it unsafe to come near. The demonstrations always troubled them; and some of them claimed that the Free Methodists would mesmerize a person if they could catch his eye—a story which others than Mormons would sometimes gravely repeat. Several of them came into the service, taking great care not to allow themselves to fall under the dangerous influence; but when there was an outpouring, and several were filled with the Spirit, thinking that devils had taken possession of these persons they fled from the place in terror, and did not stop until they were off the farm on which the meeting was held.

In the month of May, on his return to his family —who were then living at Father Sumner's—from a trip to Pine Island, Orinoco and Northfield, Mr. La Due met Rev. C. M. Damon, a Methodist minister, who had come from Iowa to visit him.

Mr. La Due, having learned through his father's letters of Mr. Damon, had opened a correspondence with him, letters of which have already been given. As a result of this correspondence Mr. Damon finally visited Mr. La Due, and during his stay of about a week their souls were knit together as the souls of David and Jonathan.

He was astonished to find that Mrs. La Due had been the wife of Rev. Wm. C. Kendall, the sainted Methodist minister of the Genesee Conference of New York; and he learned from an eye-witness something of the conflicts that resulted in the organization of the Free Methodist Church.

The revival spirit still prevailed in Cherry Valley with power, and one of the meetings at which Mr.

Damon preached lasted until after midnight. He found himself at home with these people, and felt that he ought to unite with them, notwithstanding the severe trials that would arise from such a step. While studying how he should decide this question, he went out alone on the bluff near Father Sumner's house to pray—a practice so common with the pilgrims in the valley that one farmer declared he was so troubled by the sounds of prayer and praise, in the woods and on the bluffs, that he was nearly determined to move away. While he was deeply exercised in soul, and engaged in self-examination and secret prayer, there came ringing out from the grove, some distance below him, a sudden burst of "Glory!" Unknown of course to him, and just across the road from the house, one of Father Sumner's daughters, in an agony of earnestness, had been seeking the experience of entire sanctification. Her supplication had at last prevailed, and she went to the house proclaiming her deliverance with shouts of victory. It was a place where light from heaven shone, and Mr. Damon felt very deeply the course he ought to pursue. His earnest labors since then, in the cause he once avoided, are well known throughout the church.

While Mr. La Due was still living in Cherry Valley he held several meetings in Pine Island, a town some twenty-five miles distant. Of the work there he speaks in the following letter, and also alludes to a grove meeting held in Cherry Valley:

"Pine Island, Minn., July 22, 1869.

"DEAR BROTHER DAMON: I feel like writing you. We expected a letter from you upon our arrival at Brother Sumner's last Friday, and finding none concluded you were attending the National Camp Meeting.

"Our grove meeting, held last Saturday and Sunday, was a time of great spiritual profit. Eighteen from this place attended, most of them lately converted.

"A class of twenty-two has been organized here. I never saw new-born souls so strong. Some of the gayest and wildest of this fast town have given up all for Jesus, and go shouting through the streets. Such testifying and exhorting I never heard before from boys and girls, just converted, fifteen and twenty years old. Our meetings are going on every evening. Last night a beautiful girl of fourteen found the blessing of entire sanctification. Oh, how sweetly and powerfully Jesus led her through! First, the consecration — father, sisters, brother given, all pride and fear, the world, and then unbelief. She sprang to her feet, and bounded for a spell, then lost her strength and lay for an hour looking more angelic than human; and such shouts of 'Glory' when her strength returned! Amen, Lord; so let it be. The crowded congregation was held spell-bound.

"I was positively overwhelmed with astonishment at the power in many of the testimonies and exhortations at the grove meeting. Sister Newell Sumner, in telling how the Lord had delivered her from formalism, spoke like one inspired.

"Our M. E. friends here have opened a meeting, after three years of almost complete spiritual death, under a Masonic minister. One man was forward at their meeting last evening who came forward at ours one evening and then said the way was too straight. My soul groans over this daubing, and false cry of 'Peace.'

"I am pressed with labor; but oh, glory to Jesus, 'labor is rest' in this work! What shall I do next fall, Lord, for help? O raise up laborers. Brother, If the Master has laid the cross on you of helping me on this growing work, and you reason around it or refuse it, all other crosses you may bear will only prove a hindrance to you, and a means of self-righteousness instead of Christ's righteousness.

"My soul is full. The power of the highest is upon me.

"We are about buying here a large store, the lower part to be used as a chapel, the upper as a tenement.

"Bro. Swartz joined us last Sunday, shouting and weeping.

"We are all praying for you, and send you much love in Jesus.

"Your Bro. in the war of the Lord,
"T. S. La Due."

In another letter, the next year, he writes as follows:

"Cannon Falls, Minn., June 27, 1870.

"Dear Brother Damon: We were made glad by your last; firstly, because so long a time had gone by since you wrote, that we did not know but that in these times of sudden religious changes, and somersaults ecclesiastical, you might have gone over to the side of the strong-minded and ever consistent party, who 'thank God for freedom from fanatical impulses,' and are sensitive about having much said concerning holiness as a distinct blessing immediately obtainable, but prefer to labor for 'An Earnest Christianity.'

"If the devil can contrive to make the preaching and experience of entire sanctification among us a mere general, non-particular and pointless affair, our vocation as a church is gone, and the prayer of Wesley for the Methodist body of his day, that it might be rooted out of the earth if it forgot its mission to spread scriptural holiness through the world,—this prayer will be realized in the case of the Free Methodist church most literally.   Jesus used the words, 'Be ye therefore perfect;' and through the Spirit he used the words 'sanctify wholly;' and he says, 'Whosoever is ashamed of me and my words before this wicked and adulterous generation,'—these friends of the world, these compromising formalists— 'of him will I be ashamed before my Father and the holy angels.'

"The power of God is in our meetings yet, but we have to contend for it.   The disaffected ones remain about the same.   Well, never mind; 'Our Father's at the helm.'   Glory to his name.

"The work has broken out some one hundred miles south-west of here, under a lay brother.

"Write often.

"Your Bro. in Jesus,
"T. S. La Due."

CHAPTER VII.

MR. LA DUE moved from Cherry Valley to Pine Island in the year 1870. While he lived in this place his work there was blessed, but his labors and successes were chiefly at other points. He preached in various parts of that region of the state, and also in St. Paul, in northern Iowa, and in Wisconsin.

He held meetings for a time during the summer of this year in the neighborhood of Antrim, on the prairies some distance west of Pine Island, and organized a class of fifteen members. It was here that Mother Bradley lived, whose son, Rev. J. S. Bradley, became one of Mr. La Due's warm friends, and accompanied him at times in his labors and travels on the work.

In the fall, Mr. La Due and his brother Calvin took a trip with the latter's conveyance to Iowa, where the work afterward broke out in power. From an article in the *Free Methodist* we copy the following notice of this trip, and the work at Havana, Minn.:

"PIONEERING.

"Dear Brother Mackey: We gave the FREE METHODIST, a few months ago, an inkling of a pioneer trip we made into the wilds westward, and now we write of one lately made southwestward.

"We packed a capacious box full of eatables. We were going to board ourselves by the way, and lodge wherever night overtook us and they would take 'a stranger' in. My good wife, at family prayers the morning we started, prayed the Lord to rebuke our unbelief in regard to temporalities. It seemed like a reflection on the song,

> " 'The birds without barn or store-house are fed;
> From them let us learn to trust for our bread.
> His saints what is fitting shall ne'er be denied,
> So long as 'tis written, "The Lord will provide." '

"Well, that prayer was answered, almost literally; for during a journey of three days and a half we had occasion to eat from that box only twice.

"My brother Calvin and myself went through with our noble colt, John.

"We have not time to dilate, nor our paper space for it. We cannot dwell on how we got blessed in the house of a good brother whom we found on the way, especially while climbing up above to bed on a ladder made of a single board set on one end, with pieces nailed on it, projecting each side, for hand and foot to cling to. While it swayed somewhat, we thought of Jacob's ladder.

"The result of that trip, from first to last, has been an accession to our numbers of some thirty souls, thoroughly saved—some of them backsliders reclaimed, some converts, and most of them 'sanctified wholly.' All heads of families, except two.

"We found a class at Mason City, Cerro Gordo Co., Iowa, Bro. Patrick Fay, a converted Roman Catholic, leader. We also formed a class at Havana, Steele Co., Minn., Bro. George Enney, leader. Bro. Charles Cusick, an exhorter, is supplying them with much acceptability at Havana; and my father, Rev. S. P. La Due, an ex-Congregationalist, at Mason City. My father, who some years since was much incensed at my joining the Free Methodists, we now have the privilege of receiving into the connection. May Jesus bless him, and make his last days his best.

"God has been pleased to manifest his power. A Presbyterian brother,—old-school until the late union of the old and new schools—a stalwart Vermonter, and guiltless of being of an excitable turn of mind, had to kneel on the snow on his return from a meeting one evening, and call aloud for mercy; and soon his praying was turned to loud praising. The Spirit cured all his skepticism concerning 'the power' by prostrating him on the floor one evening at his own family altar. Now he is one of the freest 'little children' I ever saw, and a staunch Free Methodist. An aged and life-long skeptic, being sick, sent for a brother at the dead of night to come and pray for him. He renounced his infidelity, warned his children against it, and telegraphed to a son in Detroit, Mich., to come to him immediately that he might warn him.

"Every lover of truth here is very much pleased with the FREE METHODIST.

"Truly your Bro.,

"T. S. La Due.

"Havana Station, Minn., Jan. 12, 1871."

During the meeting at Havana, which is the last one referred to in the above article, one man who was converted, and very soon convicted for the experience of entire sanctification, began earnestly seeking the second work of grace, but without much apparent success. He finally asked Mr. La Due to read to him something on the subject from the Bible.

Mr. La Due read a few words, when the man exclaimed, "My God! am I an infidel? Don't I believe the Bible after all?"

He then began walking up the aisle on his knees, and after going some distance suddenly arose, and said, "It's done."

A little after, the glory fell upon him, and he was sealed with the Holy Ghost. He then said that the Spirit gave him a watch-word. In the war, while in a fierce engagement, soldiers had been shot down on each side of him, and an officer stepping up to adjust something on a comrade in front of him was shot down over his shoulder. This, he saw, was the kind of warfare, spiritually, through which he must make his way to heaven; and the watch-word impressed on his mind was, "I'll stand where the bullets fly the thickest." We heard not long since of his death in Michigan. We trust that Hiram Cusick died at his post.

It was doubtless largely as a result of these meetings that a young man named Charles Tiffany was afterwards saved. His mother at this time was much blessed, and also greatly burdened for him. He attended the services, and was convicted, but did not yield until some time afterward. His labors as an instructor in Free Methodist schools, and his early death, are well known to many.

In the summer of 1871 Mr. La Due made a "quarterly meeting tour through the Wisconsin portion of Minnesota district," which resulted in extending the work. At one place on this trip he "saw the wreck of a train, the engineer of which lay several minutes crushed under his engine, while a stream of boiling water poured over his breast, he being conscious all the time. He was a young man, highly esteemed, and had just taken his place as engineer. How uncertain is life!"

He says that at another place where he stopped on this trip he took dinner at Brother Ducker's: "He and his wife used to be Troy Conference Methodists. They are longing for the sincere milk, and strong meat, and salt they were fed with of yore. They have been fed for a few years back on chalk and water, and theologic whit-leather, and white daisies, and pretty crystal gravel stones, which look like salt; but only look, and they show their fare by spiritual leanness. Brother D. got gloriously blessed some years ago at a camp meeting, near Albany, N. Y. He felt it from head to foot, and can't forget it, and can't be satisfied without more of the same kind. Sister D. told of an old sister in Troy, who was sick, who used to go a shouting to the bank after drafts on her deposits there, to be used for benevolent purposes. Oh, that there were more shouting over such use of money. Our paper and seminary would flourish and shout, then, without one plaintive note."

The following letter, written by a brother well known in the Minnesota and Northern Iowa conference, is copied from the *Free Methodist.* It describes a characteristic quarterly meeting on Mr. La Due's field of labor:

"GATHERING OF THE PILGRIMS OF MINNESOTA AT PINE ISLAND.

"DEAR BROTHER MACKEY: Perhaps a sketch of

the gathering of the pilgrims of Minnesota may be interesting to the pilgrims of other parts.

"We are scattered over a large tract of country; but Brother La Due is gathering up the scattered sheep, and therefore we are getting somewhat acquainted, consequently neglect not the assembling of ourselves together as opportunities present.

"On the 12th ult., myself and wife, together with some four children, started with oxen and wagon for Havana, distant twenty-four miles, leaving the rest of our family in the hands of the Lord, to manage affairs at home. Having arrived at Havana in the evening and attended a prayer meeting with a few of the brethren there, after a night's rest we started with several wagon loads of the brethren and sisters of that place and Clinton Falls for Pine Island, then distant thirty-three miles, leaving my oxen in safe hands at Havana. We passed through some as beautiful country as Western New York can boast of, with substantial and tasty buildings and finely cultivated farms. Arriving in the evening at Pine Island, we found Brother La Due prostrated with a threatening fever, having caught cold a few days previous. But we could not bear to see thus laid aside him whom our hearts love, and who is spreading scriptural holiness over these beautiful prairies; therefore, prayer was made unto God for him. Saturday afternoon, several loads of Brother Sumner's family came along in the rain from Cannon Falls, twenty-five miles away. Brother Sumner is the pioneer of Free Methodism in Minnesota.

"This afternoon, Brother La Due having some-what recovered, we held a sort of salvation consultation meeting. The Lord was present indeed. We found that the harvest truly is great, but the laborers few. We had made some efforts to obtain help from abroad for this field of labor, but in vain. Therefore, like the patriots of the Revolution, we resolved to use the help the Lord has given us and trust in him for success. Brother La Due preached for us in the evening. He reminded me of the apostle Paul, who preached in his own hired house. One or two years ago, he bought a building that had been occupied as a store, with a little money the Lord had placed in his hands. He did so that the Free Methodists might retain a preaching-place in Pine Island. He tore out the partitions and shelves, and seated the lower story, which is commodious, for meetings; while himself and salvation wife, and their children, occupy the upper story.

"We were glad to find a few whole-hearted pilgrims living here, who, I think, will walk the golden streets of the New Jerusalem in white. May the Lord bless and strengthen them. Brother Calvin La Due having lost his horse, steps were taken to buy him another. He will have a large circuit to travel, alternating with Brother Sumner, viz.: Cannon Falls, Pine Island, Clinton Falls, Havana, and this place, making over eighty miles in length. We had a love feast Sunday morning, and at eleven o'clock Brother T. S. La Due preached with some-what of his wonted vigor, and then we partook of the sacrament. It was a blessed time, some leaping and shouting for joy. In the evening the house was jammed full, and Brother T. S. La Due preached, and we had a solemn time. Some marked experiences were given, telling of the power of this great salvation in saving people from terribly wicked tempers and bad habits. We had a blessed time around the family altar at Brother La Due's, before retiring, which lasted about two hours. Two or three souls got out into the light of the glorious gospel of the Son of God.

"Monday morning, we had a joyful parting, bidding adieu to Brother La Due's family, and also to Brother Sumner's, who go north. We wended our way back to Havana, but some of the brethren were so full of the Spirit that they had to leap and praise God for joy on the way in their wagons, and the horses didn't appear to dislike the joyful sound. This is the kind of fanaticism we have in Minnesota.

"J. M. Cusick.

"Cooleyville, Minn."

At Pine Island were some outside the Free Methodist Church who bitterly opposed Mr. La Due, and their ill-will was so intensified by a circumstance which transpired that several of them searched the law books until a late hour one night, vainly trying to find some ground on which they could arrest him.

An old lady, whose husband died while Mr. La Due's family were in the place, feeling much at home in the Free Methodist meetings, and wishing to unite with them, asked for a letter from her church, when her son, to prevent her being received by the Free Methodists, declared that she had told a falsehood to Mr. La Due in saying that he—the son— opposed her attending the meetings. Mr. La Due took steps to have the matter fairly investigated, and an impartial committee of church members and outsiders was appointed to examine the case; but the son refused to meet the committee, and also kept his mother away. At last the old lady was so treated that she became terrified, and, climbing out of the window of her room at night, fled to Mr. La Due's and begged him to shelter her. She lived with the family some time, and both she and a daughter became Free Methodists.

The son and several others, including a Freemason minister, were greatly enraged, but were unable to injure Mr. La Due, as his conduct was blameless and he had the respect of the community.

When he removed from Pine Island he left a record clean in every respect; but, in face of the fact that he departed with his family and several loads of household goods about noon, going through the town and stopping a little on the street, it was afterward reported, in another place, that he went away at night under suspicious circumstances.

At this place, as well as in some other parts of Minnesota, the Seventh Day Adventists troubled the work somewhat. Mr. La Due took a decided and successful stand against them. A pamphlet of seventy-two pages, entitled, "Annihilationism," written by him in Minnesota, and still in print, is a good treatise against this delusion.

The most effectual check to the Adventists, however, was the presence of the Holy Ghost in his meetings. This they plainly declared to be Satanic influence; and they kept at a good distance from where the Spirit was present.

In the fall of 1871, Mr. La Due was again appointed Chairman of the Minnesota District of the Illinois Conference.

From Pine Island Mr. La Due moved to Owatonna, Steele Co., Minn. He held successful meetings in this place, and also made it the center of a wide field of activity.

One season he packed up his wide-awake lamps —made, partly after his own pattern, of tin cans which could be hung on sharpened iron rods, and designed for use in grove and camp meetings—and pushing out several days' journey into the region west of Owatonna, with his brother Calvin, held several meetings that are well remembered by many. One of his most marked experiences in this region

was at a place called Mapleton, where he held a
grove meeting which aroused much attention, and
resulted in great good.   During the meeting considerable opposition was shown by some, and a mob
attacked the congregation one night with eggs.
The eggs were gladly sold for the purpose by a
class-leader.   One of Mr. La Due's sons well
remembers the impressive services, the sudden
attack, the flying missles thrown by the mob hidden
in the surrounding grove, the indignant outcries of
the scattering congregation, and the praises of the
pilgrims amid the pelting of the offensive hail.
One young woman he noticed especially, who, with
a large, wide-brimmed hat which was dripping from
the shower that broke upon her, stood, with a kind
and shining face, thanking God that she was counted
worthy to suffer reproach for his name's sake.

Mr. La Due's brother Calvin had possibly as disagreeable an experience that evening as any one.
To preserve a new hat he had obtained, he sought
the shelter of a tree, but had just found this place
of supposed safety when a missle struck the hat
squarely, and gave it a thorough dressing.   He said
that he thought he should not try to dodge the
devil again.

Fortunately, most, or all, of the eggs were good,
and no serious damage was done.

The attack aroused the indignation of the community, and proved a great help to the meeting.

A revival of marked power afterward broke out in that region, under other workmen; the man who furnished the eggs made a public confession of the matter, sought the Lord, and was converted; and some in the ministry, as well as others among the laity, now thank God for Mr. La Due's labors in opening up that field.

At Clinton Falls, a place near Owatonna, a successful revival was held by Mr. La Due while he was yet living at Pine Island. One of those converted here was a young man who was teaching school. While the young man was seeking God one night he deliberately arose, entered the desk, and lifting both his hands cried, "Lord, I will! I will!"

The call to the ministry had been laid upon him; and as he thus took the cross, and consecrated himself to the work, he was saved. The meeting held quite late that night, and on going home he found his wife had retired. He kneeled beside the bed, prayed for her, told her what the Lord had done for him, and of the call laid upon him, and implored her to give herself to God. But when he mentioned his being called to preach, repeating his name she exclaimed, "I hate you!" and declared she had not married a Methodist preach-

er, and would never live with one. Awhile after
this, on awaking one morning, she found one
of their twin children dead beside her. This subdued her for a time, and there was hope she would
yield; but on visiting her relatives, and being
encouraged by them in her opposition, she finally
left him. He became a companion and an assistant
of Mr. La Due in a number of his travels and labors,
and has since done much for the work of the Lord.

At a meeting held in Owatonna, a man who lived
near Clinton Falls was the cause one night of
considerable commotion. The mayor being much
disturbed by his shouting, sent an officer into the
meeting, and had the man taken out and locked up.
This, however, did not mend the matter, as he still
continued praising the Lord, and exhorting those who
crowded about the place where he was confined; so
the mayor told a man to take the brother's team and
go home with him, not stopping until he saw him
safe in his own house. On the way the brother told
the man who was accompanying him that when they
reached home his wife would get a good supper for
them, and then they would have a prayer meeting
in which he hoped to see him saved. At this the
man became alarmed, and jumping out of the back
end of the wagon ran for the city, leaving the
brother to make his way home alone. The mayor

raged against the meetings, and declared he would break them up. He seemed to be under conviction and striving to shake it off. In a few months he fell into such a state of mind that he committed suicide in his own house.

One winter two young women, daughters of a Free Methodist brother, boarded at Mr. La Due's, and attended school in the city. One of them enjoyed religion; but the other was very gay and thoughtless. Much prayer was offered for her, but apparently without effect. After the rest had retired one night, Mrs. La Due was alone in the parlor, when she heard groans which seemed to come from a room at the head of the stairs. Going up quickly, she knocked at the door, and hearing no response went in. The young woman was lying on the bed dying. Great beads of perspiration stood on her forehead, her eyes bulged in their sockets, and from each corner of her mouth froth was oozing. She shook her, and lifted her up, but her head fell over, and she dropped back limp and strengthless.

Mrs. La Due exclaimed, "Oh! my God, this soul can't go from all the light that has shone in this house to hell!" Mr. La Due was away, and she called for his father, who was stopping there at the time. He hastily put on some of his clothes, and

bounded up the stairs. In an instant he noticed a
kettle of coals which the young woman had taken
with her to warm the room, and threw the window
open to let out the deadly gas and admit the fresh
air.

Regaining consciousness, she started up, crying
out, "Oh, don't let me die! I'm not fit to die!" and
rushed down stairs.

A doctor was sent for at once, and after suffering
intensely for some time she recovered. The doctor
said that she probably came within two minutes of
death.

She promised to seek God at this time, but was
soon as worldly as ever. Her sister prayed that
she might be again awakened, at any cost. Soon
after, she went to a neighbor's for water, and was
drawing up the bucket with water in it when her
hand slipped and the bucket fell quite a distance,
from near the top of the well, and the crank striking
her hand threw it into the cogs which connected
the crank and the windlass, stopping the rapid
motion short. It was necessary to take the machin-
ery apart before she could be released. For a few
minutes she felt no pain, but when sensation
returned her agony seemed greater than when she
was so nearly suffocated. Severe treatment was
necessary to save the hand, and before she could

again use it she passed through a school of exquisite suffering. After this experience she gave her heart to God.

On one of the trips Mr. La Due made from Owatonna, he held some profitable meetings at Durand, Wisconsin, a place on the Chippewa river.

In his first sermon at this place he related a little incident that brought out quite an unexpected rejoinder from a woman present.

At one time, Rev. Fay Purdy, a Methodist evangelist, was holding a revival at West Kendall, N. Y., assisted by Rev. John H. Wallace, when a woman who was known to be violently abusive at home arose, during one of the services, and made a loud profession. After she had closed, Mr. Purdy remarked, "We don't want to hear anything more from that woman until she stops throwing hot griddles at her husband." The meeting was not troubled with her any more.

It was to this incident Mr. La Due alluded in his sermon at Durand. After preaching, a woman arose who was the wife of a class-leader, a prominent man in the place. Of course she had never seen Mr. Purdy, and Mr. La Due had never heard of her. She said that she supposed she was the one at whom the story in the sermon had been aimed, but that the preacher was mistaken; it was not the griddles but the rolling-pin she had thrown at her husband. She was quite mortified at the close of the service to learn that she had made a gratuitous announcement of her family affairs.

A young man who had been notorious in Durand for his wildness and wickedness, and had been saved in a camp meeting at Owatonna, came back and prepared the way for the meetings in the former place by relating his experience and manifesting the marvellous change that had been wrought in him. He is now an able Free Methodist minister.

A number were saved and reclaimed in the meetings, and some confessions and restitutions that were made produced no small stir, as the place was noted for the stealing of saw-logs from the river.

Before Mr. La Due left Owatonna he wrote the following letter to Mr. Damon:

"Owatonna, Minn., Feb. 17, 1873.

"DEARLY BELOVED: Your last was awaiting me upon my return from my last tour.

"We are glad that you are surely, although slowly, recovering. You have reason to praise God that you have been saved from making actual shipwreck during the fiery trial of your sickness. Nothing so tests my patience and amiability as the aches, and qualms, and ennui of a sick-bed. Thank God that you have been kept by faith unto salvation, although a steady blaze of joy and glorying may have been denied you. Count your tribulations joy, and when you are tried you shall *feel* the approaches, if not the actual touches of the crown of life, in the Divine Crowner's own good time.

"The spirit of levity you complain of seems curious; but, as I bethink me, on Mondays, when my mind and body always feel unusually tired, I am often filled with a sportive spirit; and I indulge by playing with my children, even to romping and tearing around, rather to the astonishment of any anchorite. I am never condemned for it, but am quite blessed in it, in a way; it makes my Mondays quite the contrary from the proverbial 'preacher's blue Monday.' The spirit you speak of may be something of the same sort. We must be guarded, of course, and not react beyond lawful limits.

"My labors this winter have not been as productive in quantity as I could wish, but the quality is gratifying. Almost every one saved in the meetings came out very clear in entire sanctification. Praise God!

"A new secret society confronts us here, in every quarter. It is called 'The Grange,' or 'Patrons of Husbandry.' It has great fascination for the farmers, as it promises to save them much money from the rapacity of railroad, mercantile and manufacturing sharks, and to afford them valuable agricultural instruction, and high social pleasure in monthly feasts and often festivities. But the trail of the serpent of Secretism is over it all. It is an anteroom for that mystical cave, Freemasonry, and that is one of the vestibules of the pit. Its associations tend only to worldliness, and are death to spirituality.

"I was much helped of my Father in two sermons which I preached in the M. E. church in Faribault, last Tuesday and Wednesday eves. The liberal minister, Brother D—— T——, was quite elated, until he found on Wednesday that some of the pillars were quivering lest the dear church be hurt; and when I fell strengthless on the platform on Wednesday eve, after I had preached, while saying, 'My business is to preach the truth, and leave consequences with God,' then the devil ran over, and the pillars the next day muttered that I was 'filled with the devil, and likely as not a horse-thief.' Praise God. Amen. Hallelujah! The preacher had wondered why I could not preach for 'Mother' [the M. E. Church], but his wonder vanished that evening.

"Oh! I am going through, Jesus helping. Look up. Love in Jesus to you all. I am pressed, or I would write oftener and more. Pray for us. Write often.

                    "Your Bro.,
                         "T. S. La Due."

CHAPTER VIII.

S ALREADY mentioned, Mr. La Due, while living in Minnesota, was instrumental in opening a valuable spiritual field in Iowa.

A peculiar circumstance preceded his labors in that state. He and his brother Calvin were on the consecrated bluff, near Mr. Sumner's house, one day, earnestly praying for the work, when both of them were suddenly amazed to see a shaft of wondrously white light fall silently through the clear sky and descend in a south-westerly direction. They were strongly impressed that it was a sign from God in reference to his work, and that his power had gone before them and would attend them. Soon after, the way opened for them to go in that direction into Iowa, and the foundation was laid for a deep and important work. This first visit has already been referred to in the chapter on Pine Island.

In the fall of 1872 was organized the Minnesota

and Northern Iowa Conference. The organization took place "at the Stone School-house, near Plymouth, Cerro Gordo Co., Iowa," Friday, Oct. 11th, Rev. B. T. Roberts presiding.

A revival of important results was held the next winter at a school-house a few miles from Plymouth. When this revival began, such a spirit prevailed that Mr. La Due's efforts produced no more effect upon the congregation than if it had been rock. He finally called his brother Calvin out, and said they must both lay hold on God until there was a break. They kneeled down and cried for help. It was not long before the Spirit fell on his brother, who screamed with a loud voice, and was exercised in a peculiar manner. This was evidently a genuine outpouring of the Holy Ghost, for a power accompanied it that broke the strange influence which had bound the meetings, seeming literally to shatter it into fragments. From this break the work was uncommonly owned of God. Such conviction rested on the people that some screamed for mercy at their seats, trembling from head to foot; and the intense excitement which prevailed for a time was not unaccompanied by a deep work of grace, for several were converted who proved to be saints of the most marked piety and faithfulness.

Three young women were saved in these meetings, of whom at least two became specially useful. Their father was a class-leader in the Methodist Church, and they were members of his class; but this had in no way interfered with their gay attire and dancing. When the light shone on them, their conviction was deep, and the struggle severe. Their conversion and sanctification were remarkably bright. They abandoned their worldly company, and worldly dress, and served God with all the zeal with which they had sought after pleasure, at least one of them becoming a preacher and the other a preacher's wife. The mother of these young women was also converted at this time. Her husband acknowledged the next summer that he believed his wife and daughters enjoyed religion, and had been true Christians ever since the Free Methodist revival of the winter before; but after they had been saved he told his wife she could no longer live with him, sold his place to get rid of her, so that she had to go and live with one of her daughters, and, without the least ground for so doing, advertised in the public press that he would not be responsible for any debts contracted by her.

In the summer of 1873, a camp meeting was held near Nora Springs, five miles from Plymouth, during which there was for a time considerable commotion caused by some who opposed the Free

Methodists. The father of the young women just mentioned went on the stand one evening, when Mr. La Due was not on the ground, denounced the Free Methodists as "Free Lovers," and said that he had been informed by a preacher lately from Minnesota that a certain Free Methodist minister was a "black-hearted wretch," who, when he moved to Owatonna, had to leave Pine Island, Minn., at night, in order to escape arrest. The one he referred to was of course Mr. La Due. At this point, Rev. C. W. La Due, who had charge of the meeting just then, ordered him to stop, or he would be arrested. The man, who was a Freemason, called out for backers from the congregation. A crowd of Masons, and among them a number of church members, then crowded on the stand until it broke down; and others, seizing a brother who was praising God, violently dragged him about, cursing him, with oaths, crying out, "Shut off his wind!" "Club him!" "Kill him!" and repeatedly striking at him with their fists; he all the time offering no resistance, but continuing to praise God, although a man of naturally most violent temper and possessing uncommon strength to defend himself.

Mr. La Due had meanwhile been sent for, and coming on the ground at the end farthest from the stand got up on the seats, and after ordering those who were abusing the brother to stop began, with the assistance of some who were acquainted with those in the mob, to take their names. While doing this, he was attacked from behind, and knocked down between the seats, being in this way somewhat injured.

When this occurred, a strong and tall young man who belonged to the mob came forward with his coat off, and rolling up his sleeves dared any one to touch Mr. La Due again. This checked the violence, and the crowd was soon dispersed.

A pretended account of some of these occurrences was written by a Masonic infidel, who had highly esteemed Mr. La Due until he left the Congregational Church. In this article an abundance of slander and abuse was poured upon the Free Methodists, and particularly upon one of the daughters of the man who began the disturbance. It was published in the *Floyd County Press*. Mr. La Due wrote a reply which also appeared in the same paper. Awhile after the meeting, and contrary to Mr. La Due's advice, legal proceedings were begun against some of the mob; but a jury under the control of secret society influence cleared those who had been prosecuted.

Several were saved at this camp meeting, a deep interest in Free Methodism awakened through the country, and the influence of the church much strengthened.

One of those specially helped by Mr. La Due's labors at Plymouth was Hon. C. W. Tenney. He had once been converted under President Finney, and was a member, in good standing, of the Congregational Church; but at the time Mr. La Due began his revival work in Iowa was backslidden. On account of his belonging to the state legislature, and because of his influence in other respects, he was surrounded by worldly company; and he allowed himself to be wholly taken up with worldly things. On the fourth of July he took a prominent part in encouraging the tub races, and other still more hilarious proceedings, that were carried on in the vicinity; and, although a Sunday-school Superintendent, he allowed a fast horse he owned to be trotted on the race-course. As this example was public, Mr. La Due took occasion in one of his sermons publicly to rebuke such conduct, indicating, although not naming, whom he meant. He heard soon after that Mr. Tenney was quite offended. He therefore went to him, and told him that he had heard he was hurt by the remarks that had been made, and offered, if he would tell him what to say, to make a public explanation of the matter. Of course Mr. Tenney had no intention of allowing this to be done, as it would make a bad matter decidedly worse; and when Mr. La Due asked him what he thought himself of such conduct, he replied frankly, it was wrong, certainly, and that the reason of it was he had no religion. Mr. La Due's faithfulness had reached his conscience, and he turned to God with full purpose of heart. He was at last so blessed in his own house, at family prayers, when Mr. and Mrs. La Due and General Superintendent Roberts were present, that his mourning was literally turned into laughter; and having humbled himself as a little child, he became by a miracle of grace one of the few "honorable" "after the flesh" who are chosen to the kingdom of heaven.

He took off his heavy gold watch and chain, withdrew from the lodge, and, "choosing rather to suffer affliction with the people of God, than to enjoy the pleasures of sin for a season," united with the Free Methodists. His past and present fidelity and usefulness are well known.

The third annual session of the Minnesota and Northern Iowa Conference was held by General Superintendent B. T. Roberts at Plymouth, Iowa, Oct. 8–11, 1874. Before this session of the conference, an earnest request had been made that Mr. La Due come to Brooklyn, N. Y., and Mr. Roberts warmly favoring the request, he prepared to go,

For several years, in grove meetings and camp
meetings, in private dwellings and school-houses,
sometimes in city churches and again in sod shan-
ties, in summer heat and winter blizzards, he had
kept the regions where he labored well stirred for
God, and accomplished through grace results that
still abide and increase more and more. In the
all-wise providence of the Head of the Church, he
was now to remove to a new field. At the depot he
and his wife parted with Father Sumner and his
family; the one family leaving for Oregon, where
Father Sumner said he expected yet to see raised
up a Free Methodist conference, and the other to
take the cars the same day for the East.

After a short but pleasant visit with Mr. Roberts
and his wife at North Chili, N. Y., and attending as
a ministerial delegate the General Conference at
Albion, N. Y., he had changed from an itinerant's
field in the West to a pastor's charge in the city of
Brooklyn.

CHAPTER IX.

ROM an article in the *Free Methodist*, we copy the following account of some of Mr. LaDue's impressions upon again visiting New York and its surrounding cities, after his absence of years in the West:

"THE GREAT METROPOLIS.

"One of our first impressions of the great metropolis—including Brooklyn, which, while an independent corporation, is really a part of New York—is that of boundless magnitude. This is fully realized by one who travels for hours along thoroughfares flanked by lofty buildings, and thronged by a rushing crowd and thundering vehicles; and then when completely fagged, you feel that only a corner has been glanced at, and that full of suggestions of unexplored things, sufficient to occupy weeks to get any fair idea of them. Broadway is a swift, surging river of humanity and of mighty business, banked by palaces.

"Our next impression is that of tremendous

activity. It seemed like a vast heart, heaving,
throbbing, pulsating; and as we try to stop and
think of it, we are bewildered and stunned. No
time for stopping; rush on, rush on with the crowd,
or you'll be run over or drowned. The very pave-
ment stones seem to be alive and to cry out; and we
have thought at dead of night, when all might seem
still, that the ring and echo, like the moaning of the
sea-shell, had not died out of the walls of the buildings.

"Another impression is that of a mighty struggle
for life. The 'bears' and 'bulls' on Wall street sometimes push and thrust and war as though life were
at stake. The glaring advertisements, the gorgeous
show in the store windows, the startling devices to
attract attention, all seem to say, 'We must live; we
will live; give us a chance; we'll make a chance any-
way.' Ponderous wagons with many horses before
them, omnibusses, street cars, carriages and all, move
along as if for life. Everybody walks at a double
quick, none of them as if running for life, but going
into battle for it; there's just such a look on almost
every man's face—'I'm fighting here for life; no
matter who goes under, I'll have it.' The waters of
the rivers and the bay are never still, vexed with
countless keels; steamers fly; numberless sail-ves-
sels, with wide and snowy canvas, send the foam
around their bows; and an army of stout little tugs
pull and yell. The organ-grinders grind as if for
life; and the many criers in the streets cry as if life
depended on the amount of lung power they can

use, and the most outlandish way in which they can use it.

"Another impression is that of boundless wealth and magnificence; such buildings, palaces, stores, halls, institutes and churches. This magnificence is more solid than that of Chicago. The spell of astonishment and admiration which came over us while looking at some edifices there, was broken by a fall very much like that from the sublime to the ridiculous, when we were informed that that splendid cornice, and especially those statues of angels, *et id omne genus*, which peered out over porticoes and other conspicuous spots, were zinc. We could stand stone angels, and even cast iron angels; but hollow zinc angels are rather too much for our artistic sense, too much like the religion common. Here are the men worth one hundred million of dollars,—we mean in money. Here are the private mansions worth fifty thousand, one hundred thousand, five hundred thousand, one million dollars. And here, too, are the rag-pickers; the bone-pickers; the ragged, bare-footed, preturnaturally pinched, thin-faced wretches whose shivering on the cold days makes you shiver, and whose eyes, made keen like those of hungry wolves, haunt you and look you through. Here are the tenement and other houses, going down deep under ground, and touching the blue sky, where multitudes in squalor are crowded, huddled together, with brutal indiscrimination of sex, night and day.

"We look above these piles and this din, to see

what god sits enthroned as lord here, and we cannot
see him who sitteth on the great white throne, looking down and smiling, while the millions look up
and bless him; but if we see him at all it is as the
Psalmist saw when he wrote: 'The Lord looked down
from heaven upon the children of men, to see if
there were any that did understand and seek God.
They are all gone aside; they are altogether become
filthy; there is none that doeth good, no not one.'
What! no churches? Yes, hundreds of them; but,
alas! temples where pride flaunts her most gaudy
robes, and vanity minces and struts, and hireling
priests cater to the most intense and refined worldliness.

"Oh, what a field for work here! Our heart burned
at the West over the broad harvest; it burns more
here. Millions are compressed into a few miles
square, and hardly any one to hand them the true
bread. Great God, we will do all we can. Why
may not this be the metropolis of salvation and of
Free Methodism? Jesus help us."

A few were saved this year, and several substantial
pilgrims added to the society; but it was a year
chiefly remarkable as a time of trial.

A confession made by a person reclaimed under
Mr. La Due's labors, led to the exposure of two
others who had been secretly carrying on the most
infamous practices. The society was not rid of them
until they had caused considerable disturbance.

Another person was the occasion of some difficulty on account of the strangest and most unaccountable duplicity, which was not fully uncovered for some time.

Besides these lesser troubles, he also passed through another experience which was a burning, fiery furnace. He said that at times during the year, as one thunder-clap after another burst upon him, it seemed as though he could feel the hairs of his head withering at the roots, and turning gray.

One day while passing through these sufferings the scripture was strongly impressed on his mind, "One of you shall betray me." He exclaimed, "Lord, who can it be?" but was unable at that time to imagine to whom such a scripture would apply. Not long after, at a most critical time, a member of the society who had professed much love and esteem for him suddenly turned and threw the weight of his influence with the opposers, apparently thinking that Mr. La Due was going under, and that the best way to preserve his own interests was to take a stand against him.

But he was delivered, and came out as gold that had been refined, more in favor with God and his brethren than ever. The highest testimony to his unswerving fidelity, and his Christian spirit, was given by one of his strongest opposers, when he afterwards declared that if he were in a serious extremity there was no one he would rather have pray for him than Brother La Due.

His greatest troubles this year were chiefly in connection with a man then reported, we believe, to be the wealthiest man in the connection. He had called for Mr. La Due to come to Brooklyn and paid the expense of removal from the West. He was at the General Conference in Albion, and once remarked in the presence of B. T. Roberts, "Brother La Due, there is something wrong in the Brooklyn society," and added that he wished him to come and attend to the matter. Mr. Roberts asked him, what he would do if he should be the first one with whom Mr. La Due should have difficulty. He replied, "I will stand by him with my last dollar." He finally left the church, failed in business, and united with another denomination.

In the midst of these trials Mr. La Due was rejoiced to see two of his children brought to God.

During the year he had a few calls and opportunities to labor in a number of different places, in Brooklyn, New York city, at a few camp and tent meetings, once on a Hudson river steam boat when returning from the Bainbridge camp meeting, and on the work of Rev. F. H. Hendrickson—of blessed memory—in Pennsylvania.

These labors did not interfere with his regular pastoral work at the Third Avenue church.

In the fall of 1875, he was appointed to the Wilkes Barre circuit, Pennsylvania.

Wilkes Barre is a city of historic interest, on the Susquehanna river. A noted Indian massacre occurred here in early days; and the beautiful valley is the locality referred to in Campbell's Gertrude of Wyoming.

The Holy Ghost was often poured out abundantly in the meetings of this year. The services in the hall over the store of Brother Wm. B. Bertels, and at private houses, were blessed in the salvation of some souls, and in the increase of the society.

A number still live who remember with thankfulness his labors at Wilkes Barre, and at least two converted while he was there rest with him above— one of them a miner who was shortly after crushed in one of the many coal mines in that region, and who died praising God.

He preached at several other points on the circuit, especially at White Haven, a small place on the Lehigh Valley Railroad, in the mountains, where several were saved.

There were two at this place who were fearful illustrations of the danger of resisting conviction.

A sister of one of the pilgrims here was powerfully wrought upon during the meetings. Friends urged her to seek God; but, on account, it was believed, of being unwilling to make a certain terrible confession, she refused to yield, and with tears streaming down her face cried, "I can't; I can't." One night, under an almost overwhelming weight of conviction, she rushed from the house, and hardened herself against any further drawings of the Spirit.

A short time after she fell sick. At a meeting held at her sister's house it was prayed that she might be given another chance to come to God; and in the prayer it was remarked that if it was necessary for her to be kept on a sick-bed six months in order to be saved, the price would be none too great if it was effectual in her conversion. In some way the woman understood, or professed to understand, that it was prayed she might be spared six months, and then taken out of the world if she did not yield. She lingered along, sometimes confined to the bed, and sometimes able to be about. One day in the spring, some one coming along and speaking of her being alive yet, she laughed, and replied—yes, her time was not up, but it was nearly so, and she supposed the devil would be after her soon. This remark she repeated a number of different times, making sport about the prayer and her condition. Finally, as her sickness increased, she became violently profane, swearing and cursing in a manner so horrible as to confound even hardened blasphemers.

Her husband, who had likewise been under conviction and hardened himself against it, was also taken sick.. A council of doctors was called; but these were unable to render them any assistance, or even to decide what was the nature of their ailment, and declared there seemed to be no apparent cause for their condition.

The woman became so violent that her friends, worn out with waiting on her, sent for her sister who was then in Wilkes Barre. The sister found her in unutterable torments. All day she was dying, but unable to expire. The scene was too awful for her to endure any longer, and taking both the woman's hands in her own she begged God to end the agony. With a horror-stricken and distorted countenance, apparently trying to say something to the last, the woman finally ceased to breathe and her soul was ushered into eternity.

The husband jested about his condition, and with a brutal expression said he thought he would live awhile longer. But he fell into the same torments his wife had at her death, and was laid out a corpse in the same room. Both of them were buried at the same time, the coffins not being opened at the

church or the grave.   At one time in this place Mr.
La Due narrowly escaped death.   An outside section of the town, called Jerusalem, was a notorious
haunt of the Molly Maguires.   Once when going
through here, a bullet passed over his head and
lodged in a building near him.   Who fired the shot,
or for what reason, he never learned.

In September, 1876, Mr. La Due was elected
Traveling Chairman of the Northern District of the
New York Conference.   This district included eight
circuits, and extended from Wilkes Barre, Pa., into
the southern part of New York state.

The family moved to Windsor, N. Y., a town on
the Susquehanna river, not many miles from Bing-
hamton.

Several were saved this year in protracted meetings at two places near Windsor, and good was done
at various other points.

Besides attending to the regular duties of a chairman, he also made two profitable preaching tours on
the district.

On one of these, in which he was accompanied by
his wife's uncle, the late venerable patriarch of the
eastern conferences, Rev. A. G. Terry, he suffered
considerably from exposure, and his strong constitution began to show the first signs of giving way.

The other journey, in which his wife and little girl

were with him, he took with a local preacher from
Wilkes Barre, formerly a Cornish miner. They went
some distance north of Windsor into a beautiful
region on the Delaware river, in the neighborhood
of a fine farm and country retreat owned by one of
the Beechers. In this romantic, backwoods spot,
rich with honey, its hills covered with wild berries,
and its streams abounding in red-speckled trout,
was a small class of Free Methodists. A grove
meeting was held here, and several were saved.
The year, though not marked by as extensive revivals as some others, was a good one and prosperous.

The Allentown circuit, Pennsylvania, was his next
appointment, to which he moved in the fall of 1877,
and remained there two years. His work was chiefly
in the city; but he also preached at Saucon Valley
—a Pennsylvania Dutch region, where there were a
few real pilgrims,—and at Mauch Chunk, Catasau-
qua, and several other places in the Lehigh Valley.
He was also while here again elected as a delegate
to the General Conference.

In a letter to Mr. Damon, he describes as follows
one of the severe experiences of his life:

"Allentown, Pa., Nov. 6, 1877.
"BELOVED BROTHER: 'Many are the afflictions of
the righteous, but out of them all the Lord deliver-
eth him.'

"When at last conference a brother was lauded very highly by his delegate, I asked Brother Gould why he and I could not behave ourselves and obtain similar praise. Well, 'In all my Lord's appointed way, my journey I'll pursue.' 'Hinder me not, ye much loved friends'—loved, although blaming me so. I am convinced that my eye is single. The Lord gives me repeated assurances I am doing his will, our standard. Last winter, when flesh and spirit were failing, then, upon my quietly consenting to go on as straight as in the past, strength came into my bones. I was instantly cured; uncommonly good health has been mine ever since.

"Last night another assurance. Our little Mary was sinking fast with typhoid fever. After going to bed, in spirit I saw her wasting away day after day —fading, like the sweetest flower of all the universe to me, out of time into eternity. Her little hands, white and wasted, folded upon her panting breast. The night gathering upon her eyes, looking to the last the love she feels for her papa; and her voice whispering and then gasping out that love, until she lay pale, cold, motionless, dead. No tongue can tell the agony of that hour. The strong man bowed, and groaned, while every sinew and fibre of nature was on the rack. Bye and bye tears came, but that little escape of grief only seemed to put into more violent motion the flood which was pressing against the breaking heart. The deep 'oh!' was at first all that could be heard, then the sob, like the gasp for life—'Jesus help; Jesus help. Oh! my God, help or

I sink.' Then the barriers gave way, and strong cry-ings and supplications filled the house.

"Mary awaked out of her stupor and delirious drowse, and to my surprise began, in a clear tone, to comfort me. Said she, 'Papa, I am all ready. But don't feel bad; all I care about is you and ma feel-ing bad.' This only added fuel. I gave her up in will, and in affection too; but I must have a victory of glad consent. John was called from his bed. He prayed for me, and Mary and ma prayed. Soon the victory came. My mourning was turned into prais-ing. Mary was blessed. She shouted and laughed, saying, 'Oh, how sweet to love Jesus! Oh, how sweet to be blessed of him!' She fell into a profuse perspiration. To-day she is better, and bids fair to get well.

"I scanned my position while in the furnace, and saw no place to retract or change.

"*Nov. 17.* Uncommon care has prevented me from finishing this letter. Since beginning it I have known the keenest agony and the highest joys of my life thus far. The Lord knows what cords to touch in my heart. Mary has been very sick, and is yet. One night, while watching over her, and wit-nessing her suffering, I thought, can I for weeks, it may be, look on and see this? I left the room, and walked the hall and groaned. My soul was agoniz-ing. I fell on my knees by a chair, or rather over it, and begged. I acknowledged that the Judge of all the earth does right, and I kissed the rod.

"I resisted the suggestions of the devil, and in-

sisted that Jesus is all right. Soon, what revelations
poured into my spirit! I saw the love of Jesus in
voluntarily leaving heaven—where from all eternity
in the bosom of the Father he had never known a
pang, and where he might have remained forever
without a pang,—humbling himself, to suffer in soul
and body as no other being could suffer. The sufferings of Paul came before me—his pains of body,
his various pains of mind, his fellowship in experience with the sufferings of the Lord. I saw that the
most precious and mighty manifestations of Jehovah
are evinced in his power to keep these sufferers
loyal to himself in the face of their tormentors—
whether of sin, or infirmities of men, or devils,—
and to keep them glorying in tribulations also. Who
but a God could do this? The scripture was applied, 'Now no affliction for the present seemeth to
be joyous,' etc.

"The Spirit came with the truth, and oh! such
floods of grace and glory. I walked, and wept, and
shouted, and sank down under the weight.

"I have been asking the Lord to enlarge the
bounds of his kingdom in me, but little did I dream
of an answer in this way.

"I have been wrestling with death, but out of the
battle come victories such as I never knew before.

"I must know God's will by assurances as unmis-
takable as Noah and Abraham had, and then cling
to them steadfast unto the end of trial. What noth-
ings we are, good-for-nothings! How our teeth must
be pressed into the dust before God can trust us

with much of any grace! Truly God has chosen you and Frankie in the furnace—one thing after another. Well, your reward is great in heaven. Trust in God, count it all joy, and pronounce it glory. We must, we ought to; there is no other way to live in this track. Truly we are not of those 'whose portion is in this life'! Pray much for us.

"We sympathize with Frankie. ' 'Twill only make the crown the brighter to shine.' May our Lord bless you all. I will try to write more promptly. Will write soon to Brother B——. We all send love.

"Your brother,

"T. S. La Due."

During the foregoing experience, while his daughter was apparently very near death, and while he was praying for her constantly, wherever he was, the scripture was applied to his heart several times, with quiet and blessed emphasis, "The prayer of faith shall save the sick." Calling the family together, he laid his hands upon her and pleaded this promise. He believed assurance was given him that she would recover; but she still seemed sinking, blood flowing almost constantly from her mouth and nostrils. In much distress he asked the Lord what it meant, when it came to his heart with much force, "The Physician is cleansing out her system." She soon began to recover, and was restored to a far greater degree of health, and strength of constitution, than she had ever had before.

Mr. La Due did not believe that we may exercise faith for the healing of the body the same as for salvation from sin. While he held that the seeker of salvation from sin "can secure soul healing through a faith which is the privilege and duty of all," he taught that "healing is conditional on a faith specially inspired for the case," as indicated in the experience just given. He had very much faith in God, and very little faith in drugs and the common medical practice; and while he did not take the position that he would never employ a doctor or use medicine in his family, and surgical assistance was obtained a few times,—yet the family fared very well in their several experiences of sickness by the use of common sense, good nursing and earnest prayer, without ever calling in a physician.

Philadelphia was Mr. La Due's appointment for the next two years. He worked very hard here, at times, and trouble began with his lungs that ended in a few years in his death. His labors on the Sabbath were especially severe. In summer he sometimes addressed the Sunday-school in the morning, and preached afterward, held a holiness meeting in the afternoon, spoke to the crowds on the common in the evening, leading in the singing there and on the way to the church, and then preached again. During a camp meeting at North East, Maryland, shortly after exerting himself—possibly unduly so— in one of his powerful addresses before a large congregation, he had a slight hemorrhage; and his lungs from that time continued to fail until consumption ensued.

While stationed at Philadelphia he attended a camp meeting at Summerfield, Ohio, where his preaching has never been forgotten by some.

On account of his health, the society of Master street also granted him permission to visit his father and several other of his relatives, in the summer of 1881, at Fertile, Northern Minnesota.

He held a few meetings while with them, and was earnestly entreated by a number in the community to move to that region. When he left, the parting with his parents was touching. At the railroad station his father fell on his neck and kissed him.

The trip was beneficial to his health.

As has been mentioned before, Father E. N. Sumner moved to Oregon the same time that Mr. La Due went from the West to Brooklyn. He wrote occasionally after settling in that state, and finally began urging Mr. La Due to move to the Pacific coast. Feeling considerably drawn in that direction, the latter accepted an appointment again to

Allentown, at the session of the New York Conference held in September, 1881, with the understanding that if the way opened he might leave for Oregon before the close of the conference year.

The family moved to Allentown, and remained there during the winter. Father Sumner at last became so determined that he sent several hundred dollars to pay the expenses of the journey to Oregon; but Mrs. La Due's mother was too feeble to be carried such a distance. In the following spring she was taken ill, and after a sickness of some three weeks passed to the land of perfect health, free forever from the strange affliction of insanity which she had been under for many years.

For a number of years Father Sumner had been praying night and day, often with tears, for the work in Oregon. About this time he had a strange experience, which he afterward related to one of Mr. La Due's sons. He was riding one day alone on the road, his mind as usual studying over the work and his heart filled with longings concerning it, when, he said, a glorious pillar of light seemed to descend from the sky above him, and the words came to him as though uttered by a voice, "Thou art delivered."

Mr. La Due finally sent word to Father Sumner, asking if the money should not be returned, as it had been held so long. In April a messenger came to Mr. La Due's door and delivered a telegram, bearing the one word "Come," and signed, "E. N. Sumner."

There rushed in upon the minds of Mr. La Due and his wife the thoughts of separation from familiar scenes and friends, the long journey to a new country, a renewal of the conflicts and labors of frontier itinerant life, and the prospect of death in a strange land. With their children they fell upon their knees, the deep of their hearts was broken up, and with tears and supplications they again consecrated themselves to follow the pillar of fire and the cloud to the Jordan of death.

The details of preparation were arranged quickly, with uncommon ease, and before the close of the next month the family were across the continent, going by rail to Chicago and San Francisco, and from there by steamer to Portland, Oregon.

By Mr. La Due's removal from Minnesota to the East, his children had been given various educational advantages, which are always of more value than can be easily estimated. He had also seen fruit of his labors, and he and his wife had gained an experience that was profitable in many ways. He who orders all the changes of his children and his work in infinite wisdom and kindness now saw fit to remove the family to a new country and to new associations. On the journey never-to-be-forgotten kindnesses and help were given by the pilgrims at Chicago and San Francisco.

CHAPTER X.

N CLOSING an article written from Father Sumner's, near Clackamas, Oregon, Mr. La Due says: "While I write, Mt. Hood looms up before me fifty miles away but apparently not more than three, towering over two miles in the crystal air, a mighty pyramid, glistening with eternal snow. From the lowest rim my eye can see to the perfectly formed peak. It rises majestically above all around, monarch of the everlasting hills, so white, there is snow a thousand years old, so pure, awe inspiring yet glorious. It seems a fit place for the angel to rest his foot upon when he blows the trump which shall call a world to resurrection and judgment."

On arriving in Oregon, he at once began work. The Sunday after he reached Father Sumner's he preached in the Rock Creek schoolhouse, and the same week went with others some ten miles to a camp meeting being held by Rev. F. H. Ashcraft and his uncle, Rev. H. F. Ashcraft, in Powell's Valley, twelve miles east of Portland. While not considering the undenominational way in which these Free Methodist brethren were then working the best method to preserve the results of their labors and to advance the interests of true holiness, yet he found that the Spirit attended their efforts, and differences about methods did not stand in the way of Christian fellowship and his working with them.

The following Sunday afternoon, at their request, he preached to a large congregation. He spoke with characteristic power, pausing in his discourse, as we have known of his doing a few other times in his life, to sing a song of his composing, purporting to be that of the three Hebrew children in the burning fiery furnace, to the tune and chorus, "Glory, glory hallelujah! as we go marching on." In some men such an action would be affected eccentricity and stage acting, but we never heard this charge against him, even from his worst enemies. It was an unaffected outburst of his uncommon natural and spiritual force kindled by his vivid imagination and his exultant devotion. He also announced in this sermon, that he was a Free Methodist preacher, and had come to the country to stay. His unassumed, but great boldness and power, together with the announcement he made, created a stir of inquiry and interest. A Methodist local preacher went to a United Brethren local preacher immediately after the sermon, and said very excitedly, that this La Due was a Free Methodist presiding elder who had come on from the East with an understanding between him and the Ashcrafts that they were to go ahead and work into the various churches under the plea of undenominationalism, and then he was to follow them and organize. The ex-itinerant thus addressed was acquainted with original Methodism, and was not alarmed. He had been captivated with the old-time power and truth ministered by the new preacher, and replied, "Well, if La Due can take the coast with such preaching, I say let him take it!" It is true there was an understanding between Mr. La Due and the Ashcraft brethren, but it was only an understanding in the Holy Ghost. Brother Frank Ashcraft sat on the platform, his large frame, during the storm of eloquence and burning truth, frequently shaking with satisfaction and delight, and, as Mr. La Due occasionally turned and addressed himself to him, he emphatically endorsed what was said, and responded with hearty amens. Farther than this, there was no understanding between them whatever. Their first acquaintance with each other, except by report, was at this meeting.

As soon, however, as it became evident that Mr.

La Due would follow his usual course of organizing, in a regular and legitimate way, a Free Methodist work, and that some of the fruits of the labors of these brethren would go into the Free Methodist Church, the doors were closed against the brethren on every side—doors which had been wide open as long as the churches which made such an outcry against sectarianism had hoped to reap all the benefits of the undenominational movement. The basest slanders were circulated against them, even by those in high church position, and diligent pains were taken to destroy the influence and blacken the reputation of these brethren, who had been so warmly welcomed while sectarian and worldly church officials expected to play the whole work into their own hands. From annual conferences and ministerial associations, down to the pastors and lay members, a systematic war began against the holiness movement, and especially against Free Methodism. An example of the feeling raised against the undenominational holiness bands afterwards occurred in Powell's Valley. The schoolhouse burning down, the upper part of the Methodist parsonage was courteously opened for religious services, but the pastor, who professed holiness, would remain with his family down stairs, rather than attend the band services.

A prominent city M. E. preacher, and since a presiding elder, declared publicly, in the pulpit, that he could not find sanctification, as a second work of grace, between the lids of the Bible, and emphasized the expression by violently closing the book. At another time the same man, while preaching, violently closed the Bible and exclaimed that he wished he could take the word sanctification and wring its neck. Another M. E. preacher, in a neighboring city, said that all he wanted to know of any man was that he professed holiness. Such expressions as these, and outspoken Zinzendorfian teachings, flourished unreproved, and even commended, in the church which, as has been truly said, according to Wesley's account of its origin, has no apology for an existence except as a denomination raised up to advocate the doctrine and experience of holiness.

The brethren, whose work, from this time, was systematically suppressed and extinguished, labored on a couple of years longer, and then, finding the bands scattered, peeled and torn, and the church doors in every direction closed, they abandoned undenominationalism on the Pacific coast to less able and less conscientious hands, having fully proved it to be a method of holiness work unsuited to accomplish the best and most permanent results.

A number of real pilgrims converted and sanctified under their labors were glad to find a home and a shelter from the storm by uniting with the Free Methodist Church, and formed the principal part of most of the few societies first organized in Oregon. Most of those who chose to remain in the churches where they were, soon yielded to the influences around them, and although some of them retained a profession of holiness there was scarcely one here and there who retained anything more.

Mr. La Due began laboring in his old way. In the summer of 1882 he preached a few times at two camp meetings of different denominations, besides at the one already mentioned, held services in the schoolhouses around, and visited, with his wife, among the people, doing much good by prayer and conversation with the families where he stopped. One of his frequent petitions was, "Lord, give us the hearts of the people," and this request was answered here, as it had been elsewhere. Friends were raised up, and calls to work came from various directions.

In June he held a few meetings among the sailors and fishermen in Astoria, about one hundred miles from Portland, near the mouth of the Columbia river, and organized a little class, which, however, by removals, and from other causes, was soon scattered. Some of the sailors here were quite carried away by one of his original and powerful sermons entitled, "Old Ship Zion and New Ship Zion."

In July, a class of eight, including four of his own family, was formed at the Damascus schoolhouse, near Father Sumner's.

The first quarterly conference met in Father Sumner's house, November 5th, and love feast was held and the sacrament administered the next day in the Rock Creek schoolhouse.

His first protracted meeting was held five miles east of Portland in an old house which was fitted up for the services by Eugene Grantham, afterwards the leader of the little class organized there. The following account of this meeting we copy from a letter:

"Clackamas, Clackamas Co., Oregon, Jan. 4, 1883.

"DEAR BROTHER DAMON: Your last came after General Conference. It gave the only news we have had of the Conference, except that in the *Free Methodist.*

"The Brothers Ashcraft are expected here every day, may now be in Portland. I think we shall work harmoniously. Brother Roberts writes that they intend to announce themselves as Free Methodist evangelists after filling a few engagements.

"We are well assured that the Lord intends true work here. Our first protracted meeting closed last

week near Portland. We never entered on a meeting so sensible of self-abnegation, so distrustful of
self, so meek and gentle, so single in eye to the
glory of God, so full of love, so wise to win souls,
and yet we never had in some respects so fierce a
fight. I felt from the start a spirit of opposition in
one man, professing holiness, who had been very
friendly. He had professed to renounce Free
Masonry. He evidently winced at some casual
remarks I made, in a sermon, against the system.
After that I was told that he apologized to an M. E.
local preacher, and master of the lodge he belonged
to, by saying that he did not leave on account of
men like him, but because of some men who drank,
implying that he did not consider Masonry in itself
wrong. Next, some young men, great tobacco
users, came forward for entire sanctification. They
were very gently requested to give up tobacco.
The next evening they both declared there was no
sin in using tobacco, and they could use it to the
glory of God. Immediately the man spoken of
arose and said, 'Less better be said about tobacco,
and more about the blessed Jesus.' 'Amen,'
responded the young men, one of them adding,
'That man has more Christianity than all the rest
of you put together.' He repeated after meeting
the stale defence made so often,—'Why did God
make tobacco?' and he a member of the holiness
band, and professing entire sanctification! He has
a large circle of kindred, all of whom, except one
man, go with him.

"We next came in collision with the old church devil of sectarianism. You know one great cry has been on all sides, 'Away with sectarianism, it is all taken out of me.' But we surmised that this devil, in many cases, had only been laid, and not cast out. Mention of old church sins, and particularly of those of the M. E. Church, 'brings a col'ness over the meeting,' as the colored brother said speaking of stealing would over his 'meetin, cos so many ob de bredren had stole chickens.' But any allusion to the F. M. Church as better than the M. E. Church, and particularly any mention of intention to organize, provokes a hiss and a howl—an awful devil back of it. When it was evident that we would form a class, the raging began. A young man prayed before quite a congregation, 'Oh! Lord, the wolf in sheep's clothing has come. He's pokin' in his snout here and there, and it's all church, church, his church, and, oh! Lord, we hear a good many are goin' to jine the Free Methodist Church. Some are goin' to jine for popularity, and some for a great name, and some for money, and some to git married,' etc., etc., etc. Then he read, 'Judge not that ye be not judged,' etc., then Rom. 14—'Herbs,' of course meaning tobacco—of all the messes. The next evening one of them was heard trying to raise a mob against me. And all these profess to be sanctified wholly. Well, God gave us clean victory. We formed a class of six blessedly saved souls. And more to follow—one, a United Brethren preacher, one of the clearest and soundest old men

we ever met. Wife and I never felt so sweet and
strong. We are ready for another fight and victory.
One woman of more than common intelligence and
influence fell into awful darkness over opposing me
as a F. M. preacher, and was glad to come six miles
through the mud to ask my forgiveness. God will
raise up a Free Methodist Conference on this North
Pacific Coast to the glory of his name. Pray for it.

"We all send much love to yourself and Frankie
and the children. Shall we all meet again in time?
We shall, I believe, in heaven. Jesus keep us in
thine own Spirit. Blessed be his name. How good
of the Lord to call us into this way. 'Counted
worthy to suffer shame for his name.' 'In all my
Lord's appointed ways, My journey I'll pursue.'
Write often.

"Your Brother in the truth,

"T. S. La Due."

Mr. La Due continued holding meetings wherever
there was opportunity, and organizing small classes
in various places; both in Oregon and in Washington. In June, 1884, he held the first distinctively
Free Methodist tabernacle meeting in the state, at
Harmony, not far from Father Sumner's. Some
time before this he had earnestly prayed that a
tabernacle might be provided for the Free Methodist work. Shortly after, a brother who knew
nothing of this prayer came to him and said that he
had obtained a job that was bringing in fair profits,

and that the Lord had laid it upon him to buy a
tabernacle for the Free Methodist work.   The
brother sent to St. Louis, Missouri, and bought a
two-masted tent fifty by seventy feet in size, paying
also the freight charges.   Amid prophecies of
failure and expressions of contempt the tent was
pitched.   Scarce any one was found at first who was
willing to assist in the matter, and the brother who
bought the tent also furnished and hauled the
lumber for seating, and did much of the other
preparatory work.   Just after the tabernacle had
been raised, and this brother and Mr. La Due were
alone in it, they said the presence of God so filled
it that both of them were nearly prostrated, Mr.
La Due having to support himself against one of
the masts to keep from falling to the ground under
the exceeding weight of glory.   The souls since
saved in it, and the blessed annual conferences held
under its roof, are evidences that it was the Lord's.

This meeting was considerably troubled at times
by those who professed great horror of the sectarianism with which it was declared Mr. La Due was
possessed.   He seemed for awhile almost abandoned by every one, even some of his strongest
friends wavering under the storm that raged against
this attempt to organize the work, and thus put it
on a firm and lasting basis.   An opposing speech

was made one day by a Free Methodist brother
whom he asked to preach. That evening he
silently bore the whisperings of disapproval, looks
of malice, and cutting remarks that beat like a
tempest upon him from every quarter and indicated
a spirit which threatened to sweep him and organized Free Methodism from the country. He afterwards told us that he believed he had that evening
some experience of Christ's feelings before the
Sanhedrim. No rash word or hasty action, however, marred his patient endurance in the fiery
ordeal. With kindness and firmness he kept straight
forward, and when, in the course of time, the smoke
and confusion had cleared away, it was manifest
that he was right.

At another time, the same spirit of opposition
which was manifested at this meeting was so strong
in one society that a meeting was appointed at Mr.
La Due's house, without his knowledge, for the
purpose of virtually trying him and his wife on the
charges of an unchristian spirit and lying. The
meeting, however, took an astonishingly unexpected
turn, and the opposition was for that time completely silenced, to the great chagrin and mortifica-
tion of several, who soon left the church.

One of the chief causes of this confusion, and
the opposition to an organized and pure work, was

the wide-spread error of undenominationalism. One of the very ablest and most spiritual workers on this line we have ever met afterwards said, in speaking of himself and others, "We as undenominational holiness evangelists inculcated the doctrine of insubordination to all church authority." This is stating the matter very strongly, but there is doubtless much truth in the statement. And with this disregard for proper church authority too many also joined a disregard for pure church relations and right principles. With this error Mr. La Due had to contend for several years, and he said that the difficulties arising from it were some of the greatest he had ever met.

During these trials he was much encouraged by the warm approval of his course expressed by General Superintendents Roberts and Hart. In a letter to him from North Chili, N. Y., dated November 18, 1882, Mr. Roberts says:

"...one cannot in these days associate very much with even the best of the M. E. preachers without losing the keen edge off his sword, so that he hesitates about hitting such giant evils as Free Masonry and pride.

"It seems to me that you will have to do not only the work of an evangelist, but the work of an apostle in that region. It is of little use to get people saved and put them in the popular churches, or

leave them there. I am fully satisfied that the
issues which we make are Bible issues and we must
keep them prominently before the people.

"I wish you would write more for the E. C. We
miss your articles.

"I would advise you to organize a class wherever
you can find three or more who can be depended on
to be true to God and his word. It seems to me
that by next spring you should have a conference
organized for Oregon and Washington Territory.

"God bless you, my dear Brother La Due, and
make you and your family a great blessing to the
people there.

"I have not much news to write. I suppose you
have heard that Brother Tenney is very poorly, and
probably cannot live long. He is a good man and
will be greatly missed.

"The Lord is helping me, and I am looking to
him for a mighty work of grace.

"Your Bro. in Jesus,
"B. T. ROBERTS."

Undenominational leaders and bands were at this
time also springing up on every side in California.
The following letter from Mr. Hart has in it a brief
and characteristic allusion to them:

"Alameda, Cal., Nov. 7, 1883.

"DEAR BROTHER LA DUE: Yours came to hand
to-day.

"In reply would say, I think the time you mention for the organization of the Oregon and W. T. Conference the best. We shall be pleased to visit you the last of June and attend some camp meetings and organize.

"I think we have made no mistake as to the best method of introducing our work.

"We will keep plodding along and look to God to open our way. The holiness *spread* by these associations spreads remarkably *thin.* We are making some headway in this region. We arrived home on Saturday. Found all well.

"Love to all.

"Yours in Jesus,

"E. P. HART."

CHAPTER XI.

THE State Holiness Camp Meeting, conducted by the Brothers Ashcraft, was held the latter part of July at Dayton. Mr. La Due attended, and was heartily welcomed by the brethren. A number were deeply impressed by an able sermon he preached here on "The Precious Blood;" and a characteristic sermon on "Holiness and the Law," in which he laid "righteousness to the line, and judgment to the plummet," was warmly commended by Brother F. H. Ashcraft.

By the time of this meeting the churches had taken a decided stand against the holiness movement, and the ministers who had so zealously affected the brethren at first now stood afar off. A ministerial association held near by decided to have nothing to do with the camp meeting, and one minister, an opposer of holiness, attended for the purpose of proselyting, stiffly sitting on his seat during prayers, and devoting his labors to private efforts with those whom he hoped to gain. It became evident, at last, as Mr. La Due had declared from the first, that only a thoroughly organized work would meet the demands of the holiness cause in Oregon and Washington Territory.

Undenominationalism had been in such general favor at one time that even a Free Methodist class refused to attend the regular quarterly meeting, a few miles distant, and instead had an undenominational holiness band organized on that day, in which they were united with persons of whom at least some were ineligible to membership in the Free Methodist church. Mr. La Due, however, refused to turn aside from the work he had seen approved of God for years, and humbly plodded on, until a conference was organized, and, as Mr. Roberts had written him, things were put in shape for "a free field and a fair fight."

In the winter of 1884 and 1885 Mr. La Due was called upon to render assistance in a very peculiar case, much like some cases recorded by Wesley in his journal. A young married man, a member of the M. E. church, was seized at a meeting in his own house by a fit of strange and blasphemous frenzy, at the end of which he cried out, "When I leave here I am going to ——," naming a brother of this man, a Free Methodist. Just at this time this other brother was seized by a somewhat similar frenzy.

No ordinary means gave him any relief, and it was feared he would do fatal violence to himself. Finally, the first brother drove with difficulty through the crusted, and, for Oregon, the uncommonly deep snow, and brought Mr. La Due to the place. He found that natural means accomplished no good, and made the case a subject of special prayer. The father of the afflicted brother said that at last, as his son was one day about to go up stairs, Mr. La Due, who stood near, called out as if addressing an evil spirit, and in the name of the Lord commanded it to depart, and trouble the brother no more. From that hour the violence of the affliction ceased, and he was soon entirely recovered.

In February of this winter Mr. La Due baptized in his death bed and took into the church a son of Rev. E. R. Rugg, a remarkably devoted local preacher who had known Mr. La Due years before. The young man had been saved but a short time before this. His baptism was on Sunday. The following Saturday he received the Lord's Supper with a small company who were at the house, and with his sister, who lay very low in the same room. The next day he had a sinking spell in which he suffered indescribable agonies, and was at the same time terribly assaulted with temptation. The scene was too awful for the mother to witness, and she fled from the room, while the father fell on his face on the floor and besought God for help. The son came out of the dreadful struggle filled with the peace and glory of another world. The mother was called in, and at the first sight of her son's face cried out with astonishment and joy. His countenance seemed almost literally transfigured, and every one who was present declared that for about the space of half an hour it shone so as to lighten the room. On Monday morning, about three o'clock, he quietly passed away.

The brother who waited on him had entertained infidel notions, but the glory of the last hours of this death-bed scene made an impression upon him that ended in his conversion. The funeral, which was conducted by Mr. La Due at the Damascus schoolhouse, was an impressive and touching occasion. At the grave the father stood with streaming eyes and praised God for sending salvation to his family, although at such a cost.

In connection with Mr. Rugg's name the following note will not be out of place. The winter that his son died, when Mr. La Due was living at Damascus, some distance from any Free Methodists, he appeared one morning before their door with a very large piece of meat which he had carried some four miles through the quite deep snow on foot. Mrs. La Due, with tears, asked him why he had done so, when he replied that the Lord had told him to do it, and if he had told him to bring twice as much, in the same way, he should have come. This assistance came to the family in an unexpected and a most acceptable time.

The same month that Mr. Rugg's son was buried, Father Sumner ended his warfare. When he felt that his departure was at hand, like Jacob he called for his children to come near that he might bless them, and then, as he said, lift up his feet and be off. The desire expressed in the following verses of one of his favorite songs was at last fulfilled:

"Oh! when shall I dwell in a mansion all bright,
    And Jesus, my Savior, behold—
And walk by his side, like an angel of light,
    In a city all garnished with gold.

"Tho' light are the sorrows that burden his child,
    And fleeting the tempest of woe,
I long for the land that was never defiled—
    To the home of the blest I would go.

"Home of the blest, home of the blest,
    When wilt thou ever be mine?
Home of the blest, home of the blest,
    Soon shalt thou ever be mine."

The funeral was largely attended. At the grave

Mr. La Due led in singing the old pilgrim song that had echoed through Cherry Valley, Minnesota, years before:

> " Come all ye saints to Pisgah's mountain,
>   Come view your home beyond the tide;
> Hear now the voices of your loved ones,
>   What they sing on the other side:
> Some are singing of bright crowns of glory;
>   Some of dear ones who stand near the shore;
> For the fond heart must ever be clinging
>   To the faithful we love evermore.
>
> " There endless springs of life are flowing,
>   There are the fields of living green;
> Mansions of beauty are provided,
>   And the King of the saints is seen.
> Soon my conflicts and toils will be ended;
>   I shall join those who've passed on before;
> For my loved ones, O how I do miss them!
>   I must press on and meet them once more.
>
> " Faith now beholds the flowing river,
>   Coming from underneath the throne;
> There, there the Savior reigns forever,
>   And he'll welcome the faithful home.
> Would you sit by the banks of the river,
>   With the friends you have loved by your side?
> Would you join in the song of the angels?
>   Then be ready to follow your guide.
>
> " O the prospect! it is so transporting,
>   And no dangers I fear from the tide.
> Let me go to the home of the Christian,
>   Let me stand robed in white by their side."

Another patriarch had joined the seed of Israel in the Jerusalem above, and one of his daughters remarked that whenever she sang the words in the doxology, "Praise him above ye heavenly host," she thought of Father Sumner as standing among that multitude before the throne.

The Oregon and Washington Territory Annual Conference was organized June 10, 1885, at Beaverton, Oregon, some eight miles west of Portland. The tabernacle already mentioned was used. The tent was also afterwards moved to East Portland, and then to Salem, the capital city, Mr. Hart doing most effective preaching at each of these places. The following year Mr. La Due continued laboring as District Chairman, both in Oregon and in eastern Washington. At the next session of the Annual Conference he was elected delegate to General Conference. On the way he stopped with his relatives in northern Minnesota. In a letter from there he wrote as follows:

"Fertile, Minn., Sept. 21, 1886.

MY DEAR WIFE: Your good letter came last week. I sent a brief answer by card to John.

"I enjoy myself. I mean more particularly in the Lord. To be sure John and Sarah, and all the kin here treat me like a king, but my poor health has kept me in a steady fight of faith. Spells of oppressive weakness, and then returns of energy. Expectorating and coughing all the time, more than ever. Last Sunday I coughed so all through preaching that I made up my mind my preaching days were numbered. Monday morning, yesterday, I found a heavy, distressing pain in my left lung. This lung has never pained before. This pain continued until towards evening. I thought seriously that I should be forced to return home immediately, and be glad if I could even get home. I slept well last night, and feel much better this morning. Pain left my left lung. You, all, must lay hold for my body.

"Yours of the 15th inst. just came. I am glad to hear from you.

"The way opens for you into Portland very clearly.

"Well, bless God, I am feeling much better in body. Glory, Hallelujah! I'll command my children 'to do and observe all the words of this law.' I will bear *my* cross, by God's help, because 'through this' alone 'shall I prolong my days.' All write again promptly. I feel the most natural I have for weeks.

"Loving Husband and Father.

"*Sept. 22, Wed. morn.* Feel very well this morn. Currents of glory run through me. I find I am of some use when I face *my cross*, and it gives me all the work I can do. I tremble under it, and yet am strong.

"Pray mightily for General Conference.

"Good-bye,

"Father."

In a card from Fertile he says:

"I am little, but Jesus loves me. I am melted sometimes as I look towards health, my surest assurance that he favors my faith in that direction."

He alludes in the above remark to what he considered an assurance in regard to his health. To this, many know, he clung to the last. We are confident that in this case he fell into the very natural and innocent error, against which we have sometimes heard him guard others, of mistaking a blessing received while praying concerning something for an assurance in regard to it. Several other assurances he claimed during his life, and in reference to none of them do we know of his being mistaken. Concerning their fulfilment he seemed confident in the darkest hours. In regard to the recovery of his health at this time, he never appeared to have that confidence he had shown in other instances; and he was sometimes sorely troubled with the thought that possibly his not recovering was owing to a lack of faith on his part, or of a failure to meet the conditions of faith. That there could be such a lack after his glorious triumphs in the past, and at a time when his whole being, as never before, was swallowed up in God, is to us incredible. He was at times, however, sorely tempted that this was the case, and his temptations were doubtless unwittingly increased by the well meant but mistaken kindness of some who leaned toward the doctrine of entire exemption for

the people of God in this world from all the physical as well as the moral effects of the fall.

He loved life, and at funerals, in speaking of the
remarks that are occasionally made about the beauty
of some corpses, we have heard him say that he
thanked God there was a world where there were no
such beautiful sights. Every death was to him a
kind of public execution, and an awful testimony of
the nature and consequences of sin, and while he
longed for eternity and the last, great day, yet, with
his intense imagination, he sometimes trembled at
the thoughts of the dreadful conflicts some dying
saints have had with pain and the powers of darkness. Much of this he was spared, and doubtless
one mitigation of the suffering was his not expecting death when it came.

Elisha received a double, or at least a first-born's
portion of the spirit of Elijah, who was translated;
and even his dead body raised a man to life. If we
are to judge from the scripture account of him, his
path was that of the just, and shone "more and more
unto the perfect day." Yet "Elisha fell sick of the
sickness wherewith he died." So it was with Mr.
La Due. We can say of him, he prayed for health
and opened his eyes in immortality. "He asked life
of thee, and thou gavest it him, even length of days
for ever and ever."

He reached Coopersville, Michigan, Oct. 14th, where he was assigned a pleasant stopping place with Mr. Lily, the postmaster of the city.

He rejoiced here to meet again with Mr. Roberts, whom he had prayed to see once more in the flesh, if it was the Lord's will. He was also glad to see Rev. C. M. Damon, Rev. William Gould, Sister Jane Ray, and many other friends, from whom he had been separated for some years.

He was greatly touched by the kindness shown him on every side.

But what gave him the highest satisfaction was the evident purpose of nearly all who represented the church to abide by the ancient landmarks of scriptural doctrine and discipline, and to welcome among them the presence of the Holy Ghost. He was satisfied that the work of the church was on the whole deeper, wider and more spiritual than ever.

His health was a source of considerable trial to him at the conference, but notwithstanding his increasing weakness he filled his post with ability and faithfulness, serving on some important committees, taking part in the business on the conference floor, and preaching with impressive spiritual eloquence and power.

On his way home from General Conference he

again stopped with his relatives in northern Minnesota. In a letter from there he writes as follows:

"Fertile, Minn., Monday, Nov. 1, 1886.

"My Dear Wife: I reached here Saturday on the cars. Found all well. Great R. R. excitement. New city building up.

"I am holding on for health and life. Expectorated more blood last Saturday morn. than ever before at any one spell. Have felt better since— not so much suffocation.

"Preached twice yesterday. Had blessed liberty. Last eve. nearly all in the congregation arose signifying their desire for the religion I preached. I preach again Wednesday eve., and perhaps through the rest of the week, and next Sunday morn. and eve. I am making no provision for the flesh, not looking at pains, but unto Jesus my Resurrection and Life. I feel better 'to have faith and stick to it,' as Mother Wallace said.

"I expect to be at Cheney, Friday the 12th.

"I sent a letter on Friday last from Minneapolis to William, enclosing N. P. Ex. money order of $25.00. Do you have enough to make a live? I subscribed for La Due and sons $5.00 on the new publishing house. Presently Brother Coleman put a bill in my hand, which I found to be a X. The next day a brother gave me $5.00 more.

"Thirty and more of us went to Grand Haven, found the steamer would not leave until the next night. We all took the cars, Brother Arnold asked

me to share his double berth in the sleeper, which
I did with much comfort.

"I hope the boys may hold some protracted meetings.

"Remember, I live by your prayers. Love to all.
"Yours most affec.,
"T. S. La Due."

From Fertile he went again to eastern Washington, where he held several successful series of meetings in various places. As he stepped from the
train in East Portland, December 31st, the son who
met him at the depot could scarcely refrain from
weeping, for his face seemed evidently to bear the
stamp of death. He did not attend the watch-night
services, but the next day preached twice in the
W. C. T. U. hall, which the little society had rented.

He remained in East Portland several weeks,
preaching a number of times, and greatly strength-
ening a few saints who were struggling on amid
many difficulties.

On account of his faithful stand against secret
societies, and some other evils, some abusive mis-
representations, accompanied in one case with slang
epithets, were at this time published against him in
a disreputable secular paper, and also a religious
periodical circulated extensively on the Pacific coast.

CHAPTER XII.

HE NEXT session of annual conference was at Dayton, Oregon. Mr. La Due was unable to attend, being confined at the home kindly given him at that time by Brother Eugene Grantham, five miles east of Portland. He was wasted away until all his bones stared upon him, and panting from shortness of breath, and swooning when trying to walk from his bed to his chair. Mr. Hart and his wife visited him on their way to the annual conference, and bade him farewell, not expecting him to live more than a few weeks. He had at this time a severe struggle, suffering much both in mind and in body, but he laid hold upon God, and by his faith, his determination and the blessing of the Lord rallied so much that when his son returned from conference he found his father quite a different man.

In the latter part of July he was able to go to East Portland and conduct a testimony meeting; in

August he preached there in the house of Brother
Daniel Long; and in September he made ready and
went to Puget Sound, holding a number of meetings
there, and not reaching home again until the 23rd
of October. He returned home feeling considerably
better than when he left. The last quarterly meeting
he held was at Independence Hall, November 13. He
could scarcely stand, and read the sacramental service with much difficulty, but the glory of God was
manifested in the place, especially, as was often the
case under his administration, at the Lord's supper.

His last discourses were three different sermons
from the closing words of the 139th Psalm, "The
way everlasting." The first of these sermons, we
believe, was delivered before quite a large congregation at his last quarterly meeting, in Independ-
enc Hall, a few miles east of Portland. The others
he preached in the house of Brother Daniel Long,
in East Portland. At the first of these two sermons
in East Portland a young man of some ability was
present, who had been stopped in a course of dissipation by a sudden stroke of paralysis. He was
deeply wrought upon at this service, weeping, and
declaring his purpose to live for God. It is to be
hoped that through the influence of this meeting,
and other means, this young man was saved before
he left the world,

The service just mentioned was held in the morning. That evening Mr. La Due felt so weak that he did not know but his son would have to take charge of the meeting, but he rose, with difficulty, from the bed, made his way feebly into the other room, and sitting down preached what proved to be his farewell sermon. When he began he suffered from shortness of breath, being hardly able to speak above a whisper, and expectorating very much. He stopped, and told the pilgrims to look up for him, when, almost as soon as the request was made, the Spirit came upon him, and he shouted, and praised God. He then went on, with a full, strong voice, and preached at least as powerful a discourse, we believe, as he ever delivered. The weight of the Spirit that rested on him that night was different from, and exceeding, anything we have ever witnessed. The little room was a place awful to the unprepared, and solemn, but glorious, to the saved. Eternity was seen and felt to be so near at hand that it almost seemed, at least to one who was there, that the sounds without were already the gatherings of the final storm, that the signals of the river boats were in a moment more to be followed by the blast of the archangel's trump, and that the great white throne, with all the realities of the judgment day, was ready almost immediately to burst upon the

world. The last two or three months of his life he had
some severe conflicts. He was troubled with the
thought that he might be burdensome on account of
not being able to go out on his work. He was also
tempted, as we have before mentioned, that his not
recovering might be from lack of faith on his part;
and, besides these trials, he was called upon, at this
time, to drink probably the bitterest cup of his life
because of the spiritual condition of two of his
children. But he was triumphant in faith, being so
filled with glory at times as to praise God in a way
that would seem impossible with one so far gone in
consumption. He studied the Bible much at this
time, and read considerable in a cheap edition of
several standard works of literature he had been
able to buy, especially in Geikie's Hours with the
Bible. He remarked one day that the enjoyment
of good books, of food and of home was about all
the pleasure we could have in this world outside of
grace. He was favored with a good degree of these
pleasures almost to the last hour, and the blessing
of the Lord was given him so abundantly that he
said he believed he would be willing to suffer on for
years, if there was no other way by which he could
be given such a measure of the Spirit. From
an article written by his wife, which appeared
in the *Free Methodist* of, April 18, 1888 we

copy the following account of the closing scene:

"Most of the time for the last two months, while we were living with Brother Eugene Grantham, it was his habit to rise about 5 o'clock, and as soon as the fire in his room was made and his morning toilet was over, to sit down beside his own lamp in his rocking-chair, and read his Bible for an hour. He was committing to memory the whole of Hebrews. These morning hours were to him the richest of the day, and he often said, 'You little know how sweet is the word of God. It is literally sweet to my taste. It is sweeter than honey in my mouth!' Not one of us doubted his assertion. A holy quiet reigned in the house at that hour. At family prayers he often prayed through to the throne, and our neighbors knew we loved praise as well as prayer. His shrill screams of victory and loud hallelujahs will long ring in our ears. These bursts of praise never tired, but rested him. Perhaps it was in this way he kept able, almost to the last hour, to dress and undress with but little help, and get in and out of bed every day.

"The first week in March, he had planned to return to our old home in Powell's Valley, on Brother Robertson's place, so kindly given us as a home, besides much of our support for the last four years, and where we had enjoyed the presence of God in great power in our weekly meetings. It had been a place of rest after weary rides over Oregon roads, and to it he turned again, to rest among the fruit-trees awhile. He had planned himself all the

needed repairs for the house, and the packing and
loading of the most of our goods. All was done as
he wished by our good brethren; and when Brother
Grantham endeavored to have him wait a few days
until he was stronger, he insisted that he should be
taken on a bed in a covered spring wagon the next
day, March 7th. We had a beautiful day for the
trip, and he seemed so to enjoy the sun and fresh
air. I was wonderfully encouraged, even in the face
of symptoms that are considered sure proofs of a
consumptive's death. I said to him, 'Do you know
that all the signs are against you?' He said, 'Yes, I
am getting very familiar with the last stages. But
what does it matter? If I go it will be a most
glorious surprise, and rest would be so sweet after
such a long and fearful struggle for life. But I
shall live, and not die.' So he was permitted to
hope on, and keep up courage to the last.

"When we reached Brother Robertson's, for the
first time he had to be lifted and carried to the bed,
and yet affirmed he was better for the ride—it was
about eight miles, and a good road most of the way.
When once laid upon the bed he said, 'What makes
it seem so like Heaven here? There is so much of
Heaven here!' He ate quite a hearty supper, but I
noticed he neither coughed nor raised from the time
we left Brother Grantham's. He insisted that night,
as he had before, that no light should be left burning, and that all retire. I waked twice in the night
and found him quiet, yet speaking of severe pain
in his back. In the morning he called for some

custard, but insisted we should '*Have prayers first*,' before he ate. [At home he usually had prayers after eating. Sternly, and yet kindly and prudently, faithful, even in death, he evidently wished to teach a lesson which he knew was then—but, we believe, is not now—needed, by thus making sure that prayers should be held, and that all should be present.]

"He lay very quiet till nearly noon, asking me once to talk to him, and then wished to be taken up into a rocking-chair. When lifted into it, he found he could scarcely breathe, and called for the doors to be opened, and then closed, several times. Soon he called for us to put him back upon the bed, and then became apparently so paralyzed he could hardly speak. Before this he had asked us all to pray. He asked the second time, saying, 'Pray, pray,' and while we did so Brother Robertson was so overwhelmed he could scarcely keep his position. The glory came down like rain, and although husband could not speak his eyes and every feature so shone with the light from the other world that I felt the hour of his translation had come. There was a clearness, a radiance in every feature, as his eyes wandered through the room, all absorbed with some heavenly vision, that told, more than words could, of the 'weight of glory.' He threw up both hands and began to breathe hurriedly and deep, as if to make sure of something important. His expression was as if closing up one of his most powerful sermons, the same expression of the

mouth; the eyes bright and glistening.   All at once
the hands dropped, the eyelids began to fall, and
the breathing grew softer and fainter, till not a
motion or sound could be detected.

'So gently shuts the eye of day,
So dies a wave along the shore,'

was all I could think of. So gentle! So like the
end of a righteous man! As I stood holding his
hand, and eagerly watching for the last golden ray
that glimmered through the opening gates, I felt
but one thing impressed by the Spirit, and could
only shout through my tears, 'Good is the will of
the Lord.'   I think I never before stood by a death-
bed where there was so little sense of death, and
such an overpowering sense of divine love.   The
air was so fragrant with love, that we were melted
down before the Lord.   Numbers could not believe
that he was dead; his face was so like a quiet sleep.

"I know I have lost a fond and faithful husband,
and as a family we have lost a fond father, a true
and safe counsellor.   He had but one purpose, to
lead men to Christ; but one aim, to be true to God.

"We as a family, who knew his every-day life,
can witness that in every important case he waited
on God, prayerfully, till he understood the mind of
the Spirit, and did not fail, when he knew it, to take
up the cross that was sure to be followed by the
inward glory.

"Brother Scott of Seattle, was secured to preach
the funeral sermon at Powell's Valley, in the Baptist

church. His text was from Rev. 14:13. God wonderfully blessed, and helped him to present the
'narrow way' as the only safe and glorious way. It
was a glorious season to all the saints; and a large
congregation was moved to tears while Brother
Scott told them that in their hearts they knew that
Brother La Due was right, and loved their souls,
and had gone where he would be more popular than
he was here, while preaching to them the plain
truth.

"I ought to mention the deep interest he felt in
the work. But for the severity of the weather he
would have visited the Walla Walla district in February. An appointment was out for a meeting
about one hundred miles south of Portland, and his
satchel packed to attend in a few weeks. He was
never before so alive to the interests of God's cause.

"MRS. M. F. LA DUE."

CHAPTER XIII.

IN THIS chapter will be found recollections of Mr. La Due, and estimates of his character, furnished by several of his intimate friends.

Rev. C. M. Damon sends the following:

"Orleans, Neb., Apr. 8, 1890.
"Rev. J. La Due:

"My dear Brother,—I am greatly pleased to learn that there is prospect of some memoirs of your revered father being soon given to the public. The intimacy of my association with him for several years was such that I may perhaps be pardoned for communicating a few incidents or thoughts additional to those elsewhere appearing.

"His chief characteristics, as they appeared to me during a long and valued friendship, were purity and integrity—great purity of personal character, and fidelity to the truth and will of God, answering to the poet's 'faith,'

" 'That bears unmoved the world's dread frown,
Nor heeds its scornful [or seductive] smile.'

"During the years of my acquaintance with him
I judge that no one ever heard him, in private life,
utter a word, or saw him manifest an expression,
the Christian propriety of which could be seriously
questioned. Certainly this was my experience.
His rebukes of formalism in public were often
scathing and exposed him to the opposition of
many; but a more meek spirit, self-poised and
calmly stayed on God, it has never been my privilege to meet. He did indeed fear the 'friendship
of the world' to an extent that some might deem
extreme. Remarking on certain revival services
where the fruits were not readily apparent, he
observed, 'If one does his duty, the people will soon
fall out with their sins or with the preacher.' On
another occasion, where results differing from the
above appeared to follow labors of marked ability,
he publicly uttered the caustic criticism, 'woefully
popular.' But whether or not one coincides with
the sentiment thus expressed, it was manifestly
born of the deep convictions with which he was led
to feel that every act, and every word, especially of
one divinely called to the ministry, is naked and
opened to the eyes of him before whom we are soon
to stand in judgment. From the profoundest depths
of his soul he prayed,—

" 'And O, thy servant, Lord prepare
A strict account to give.'

"The circumstances of my first acquaintance with

him were by a singular and interesting train of
providences. Having been, while a member of the
Methodist Episcopal Church in the state of New
York, awakened to the subject of entire sanctification, and with considerable sense of its practical
bearings, I had as a professor and advocate of its
experience, sought to avoid complication with Free
Methodists by a change of residence which I
supposed would place me far beyond any knowledge of them in that early period of their history,
and so enable me to act untrammeled in my church
relations. It was strange that within a month after
my removal to Iowa I should have accidentally
met, in the person of Rev. S. P. La Due, a highly
respected and very genial minister of the Congregational Church, your esteemed grand-parent, and
thereby laid the foundation of an acquaintance
which was so soon to exert a powerful influence
over my personal relations and life work. Of this
acquaintance and its interesting results I made note
some time after in a tract entitled, 'Why I am a
Free Methodist.' Suffice it to note here that
through this channel of influence, and from seeing
an article I had published in the *Guide to Holiness*
embodying the intense convictions with which as a
young minister I was then struggling, a letter was
addressed to me some months after, and at a time
of great susceptibility, by your father, the opening
sentence of which, 'I write you, first, because I feel
God leads me to,' penetrated my soul with a
pungent sense of communication with one accus-

tomed to walk with God and act under a realization of his immediate presence.

"I visited him by permission in the spring of 1869. He was in charge of a society in the valley of the Little Cannon in Goodhue Co., Minnesota, which became the nucleus of the Minnesota and North Iowa Conference. Among the features which riveted my attention in my sensitive state of mind and heart were his deep and genuine spirituality, his intense opposition to religious formalism, and the fact that, coupled with those elements, he *studied* to show himself 'approved unto God, a workman that needeth not to be ashamed, rightly dividing the word of truth.' I noted this the more closely having been previously impressed with an understanding that I was about to meet a minister of marked ability and one of much promise in the denomination with which he had been formerly connected; also, perhaps, because of a certain curiosity to know whether a loose and ranting style was to be inevitably associated with a high reputation for spirituality. I was pleased to note that while there was no ostentation of learning, or affectation of scholarly bearing, he did not, on the other hand, though amid the rude surroundings of a pioneer life, lower the becoming dignity of his ministerial profession by affectation of bluntness and neglect of sober, earnest study and wise method in preaching.

"Another point of much importance, which may be overlooked by others, permit me to note. I refer to the scrupulous, though not offensively con-

spicuous, care with which all his ministerial relations to the opposite sex were governed, by which
he was enabled, in a time and under circumstances
of peculiar liability, wholly to avoid the breath of
suspicion and maintain an untarnished reputation as
a minister of our holy religion. He was in this
respect, as in many others, truly an example to his
younger brethren. No word of jesting escaped his
lips. No 'unseemliness' of conduct marred the
purity of his intercourse with the flock of Christ.
With quiet and unobtrusive demeanor he would
even choose his seat in riding to avoid unnecessary
contact, and thereby forestall the possibility of
unfavorable remarks.

"His personal habits were in a marked degree
free from extravagance. He was truly in all his
private intercourse a gentleman; if not by nature,
made so by the Spirit of Christ. The influence of
his pure life was, the recollection of it still is, as the
breath of heaven. Yet, like the gentle and 'beloved
disciple,' he was Boanerges, a son of thunder. The
flashing of his eye, accompanying the peal of a
powerful voice, as with majestic sweep and stalwart
stroke of the Spirit's two-edged sword he strove to
cleave down the man of sin, as one 'set' of God 'for
the defense of the gospel,' revealed the lightnings
of divine wrath and struck terror to the heart. He
lived for eternity. The world knew him not, as it
knew not Christ. We have known men to sneer at
him as a fool after some of the most brilliant and
powerful sermons to which we ever listened. His

reward is with the Lord.   He was eminently sound in doctrine.   While he did not affect to be a theologian, he was one in reality.   His valuable pamphlet on materialistic Adventism attests this fact.   Some of his sermons were powerfully theological, as well as keen-edged and spiritual.   In the early part of our correspondence he wrote, 'I was made a John Wesley Methodist in doctrine and experience.'   He was such in truth.

"He was sound in faith.   The loud and peculiarly intonated 'Amen' which frequently interrupted his own petitions, even at their beginning, and often followed the utterance of some radical truth in preaching, and which he interpreted as the Spirit's endorsement of such truth, became a powerful second to his words on such occasions, and was attended with a marked uplifting of the faith of his hearers.   The conviction produced was as of one who walked with God and enjoyed familiar, though reverent, access at the throne of grace.

"Yours in truth,
"C. M. Damon."

Rev. Wm. Gould, who was Mr. La Due's district chairman several years, both in New York state and in Pennsylvania, writes of him thus:

"Brother T. S. La Due.

"The thought or mention of that name brings out from my memory-album a face associated with precious recollections. I saw it first at Whitewater, Wisconsin, in the fall of 1870.

"Among a group of brother ministers and laymen of the Illinois conference having a photograph taken, stood a tall, thin form, surmounted by a head, the side-face view of which bore so much resemblance to that of the then recently martyred president of the United States, that I called the attention of a bystander to it and asked, 'Do you not see Abraham Lincoln among them?' He replied, 'Sure enough; that is old Abe.'

"Subsequently I saw him in his throne—the pulpit, and listened with delighted ears and overflowing heart to such a scriptural, brilliant, burning, inspired, spiritual and unctuous outpouring of gospel truth, from the words 'The love of Christ constraineth us,' as revealed to me that I was listening to no ordinary man.

"I had previously heard Beaumont, the Methodist Demosthenes of England, Spurgeon, now of world-wide fame, and many other men of great pulpit power in the land of my birth. I had listened to Beecher,—then in his prime—and Talmage,—a rising star in those days,—with other preachers of great fame on this side of the Atlantic; but I at once gave Brother La Due, in my mental estimate, a high seat among the best of them as an *able* minister of the New Testament from the literary standpoint, and as especially eminent in the ministration of the Spirit, in which some of those I have alluded to were—as I think—lacking.

"Nor did my subsequent and closer acquaintance with Brother La Due compel me to alter my estimate; for while he did not always rise in his pulpit ministrations to the glorious altitudes he sometimes touched, yet, again and again, I have sat and gazed, with his congregations of spell-bound auditors, while he soared in his uttered contemplations of God and things divine, to heights seldom reached by ordinary preachers; and listened, at times almost breathlessly, while he poured upon us, out of his illuminated heart, the truths he saw and felt in those moments of mental and spiritual inspiration; feeling meanwhile, most unmistakably that he was a veritable New Testament prophet.

"I first admired and enjoyed the *preacher;* but subsequently, soon and increasingly I became acquainted with and loved the *man.*

"Some time later, he united with the conference of which I was a member, and I was brought into close relations with him as his chairman and otherwise.

"He was emphatically 'a man of God.' In him, the image of the Master could not merely be traced but *shone.* Humble and childlike in spirit, unassuming in demeanor, guileless, open and frank, an intense hater of sin, a determined enemy of all iniquity and of all compromise therewith, he possessed the rare quality of integrity in a high degree.

"He did not sit on the fence, and was always to be depended on to work and vote for whatever he believed to be right. Were I intrusted with the conception of a heraldic emblem expressive of his character, I would suggest, a lamb couchant, and a lion rampant; for while he was meek, and of a quiet spirit, he was also bold and daring in the cause of truth. He feared not to espouse a cause simply because it was unpopular. He stood up to be counted without looking around to see who else was standing. Of him it may be truly said,

> " 'He dared, had heaven decreed it, to have stood
> Adverse against a world, and singly good.'

"In dealing with souls he showed fidelity to principle, and the blade of truth he used, though wielded in love, cut to the quick; hence, he sometimes offended and brought persecution and unpopularity upon himself, as did his Master, who spoke as never man spake, his enemies themselves being judges. All men did not speak well of Brother La Due; but many will bless God forever for the faithful dealing of his servant with their souls.

"It may be that he, as well as some others of like nature, would have been made more efficient by learning more lessons in prudence, cautiousness, and even in loving forbearance. It is possible that intense dislike of evil may beget a resistance that is not sufficiently temperate, and a zeal in opposition not wholly wise. Not many of us know how to use the 'scourge of small cords' aright, or how to pronounce the woes on 'scribes and Pharisees' in just the spirit of the Master; but in these days of sickly sentimentalism, emasculated love, nauseous sweetness, and untempered-mortar daubing, the advent and operations of a man like T. S. La Due are as necessary and helpful for the destruction of moral and spiritual miasm, as that of thunderstorms in the natural world, when the atmosphere is stagnant and charged with pestilential vapors.

"In thinking of him, the writer is reminded of the superlatively meek Moses, when he broke the tables of the law, pulverized the golden calf and made the people drink the water embittered by its dust; of the gentle Samuel, when he hewed Agag in pieces; and of the loving Paul, who, though he could wish himself accursed for his countrymen's sake, could and did pronounce the 'Anathema, Maranatha.'

"Dear Brother La Due is gone up. Had he been less outspoken and faithful he would have been more popular; but would his Master have said, 'Well done?'

"May his mantle fall on some Elisha with a seven-fold increase of his spiritual and intellectual power. Amen.

"W. GOULD."

We close with a few words taken from a paper sent to Mrs. La Due by Hon. C. W. Tenney, to which paper we have been indebted for information already used in the preceding pages. In explanation of part of what he says, we note that Mr. Tenney and his father had lived at Oberlin, Ohio, where they were acquainted with Mr. Finney. They afterward moved to Iowa, where Mr. Tenney met Mr. La

Due when they were both young, and finally married
one of Mr. La Due's sisters. He says:

"He, as a young man, possessed a power to
attract and interest others that I have hardly
ever seen equalled; and when it was used for their
advancement and improvement, it gave him a wonderful influence over all with whom he came in contact. I have often heard this spoken of by those
who met him for the first time.

"He was very fond of conversing with my father,
who believed in the doctrine of holiness, and had
that experience, though not generally endorsed and
understood by the Congregational Church. He was
fond of reading the works of the late Charles G.
Finney, and talking of him, and knowing that I was
personally acquainted with him, asked me his views
on several points relating to holiness. I was hardly
prepared to answer his queries authoritatively, and
said to him, 'Mr. Finney is still alive, why do you
not write to him personally, and ask him?' He
replied, 'Do you suppose he would deign to notice
such an one as I?' I answered, 'Most assuredly he
will; and I'll send a letter of introduction.' At our
next visit he informed me that he had two letters
from Mr. Finney that were very satisfactory. This
was near the time when he went to St. Charles, Illinois.

"This brings me to the time, dear sister, when *you*,
better than anyone else, know his subsequent history and labors. How, under the Lord, he was a

blessing to me, and by his faithful life, example and counsels, won me back from the paths of formalism, to repentance and the new life. How he guided that dear sister across the dark river, shrinking not from the truth, until she could see the way, and almost the lights of the Golden City. On the few visits he was permitted to make us later, you accompanied him, and have probably included that portion of his life in what you have prepared.

"I recall the two sessions of General Conference —the one at Spring Arbor, Michigan, in 1878, and the other at Coopersville, Michigan, in 1886. At the former, I had the pleasure of rooming with him all through the session, and I could not but notice the deep, firm trust in God, and the calm and saint-like expression of his countenance. I remember at one time, when a matter in which he was deeply interested had been decided contrary and adverse to his expectations and desires, one of the brethren who entertained similar views, and who also had been disappointed in the decision, approached him expecting to find him somewhat unsettled and disturbed, and exclaimed quite earnestly, 'Well, Brother La Due, what are you going to do?' With that sweet smile so peculiar to him, he looked up and cheerfully replied, 'The Lord reigneth!'

"At Coopersville, though in feeble health, he was always in his seat, carefully watching everything that transpired, and occasionally speaking a few weighty words, showing a clearness of perception seldom observed. His opinions were treated with marked deference; and when, near the close of the conference, it was announced that he would preach in the Free Methodist church, the house was packed to its utmost capacity, and many left who could not find an entrance. The Lord seemed to give him strength and special help for the occasion. With prophetic eye, he seemed to see some of the rocks on which the church might be stranded or wrecked, and warned them faithfully of the danger. He held the large audience with breathless attention for an hour and a half, and as he took his seat, I remarked to my wife, 'That is brother Thomas' dying charge to the Free Methodist church!' A few days later in Chicago, as we clasped hands at parting, he said, 'Well, brother Charles, if we never meet again on earth, I shall expect to meet you around the throne!' I felt a presentiment that I might never see him again here below.

"Since I learned of his peaceful departure, I can, in imagination, see him with that company that John saw, who had come up through 'great tribulation.' He rests from his labors; but his work still goes on, and eternity alone can disclose the final results of his faithfulness. His has been a 'good fight;' his 'course is finished.' He wears the crown of the faithful, and now enjoys the full realization of that blissful rest he often so vividly pictured to our view. May we all clasp hands on the other side of the river in that City of Gold, is my prayer.

"Yours in Jesus,

"C. W. TENNEY."

SERMONS

AND

SKETCHES.

SERMON I.

"Precious in the sight of the Lord is the death of his saints."—Ps. 116:15.

EATH is a powerful testimony from God of the distress, ana woe and pain caused by sin. Death is regarded by man, and pronounced by God, the most bitter evil of earth.— Gen. 3:17–19. The chief aim of man, in a very essential sense, is to preserve and prolong life and escape death. For this we eat, and drink, and dress, and build, and spend the most of our time and labor.

How sickness is dreaded! Great concern. Physician called. Report of the case. Alarm. Then every symptom watched. The sinking. The mortal struggle. The last gasp. Gone! "Beautiful in death:" thank God, there is a world where there are no such spectacles of beauty.

God stands by every corpse, every grave, and reads Rom. 5:12: "By one man sin entered into the world, and death by sin; and so death passed upon all men, for that all have sinned."

The death of the saints is a more weighty demonstration of the awful nature of sin than the death of the sinner. God says, "See, I am so bent on showing to all men, and to the universe, the terribleness of sin, that I will not spare even my saints, my holy ones, the death of the body and the agony which comes from losing friends."

Death is a testimony of God against sin, even the death of the saints. We need not be startled at this statement in regard to the death of the saint; for God has in no way so expressed himself against sin as by the death of his Son. The death of billions of fallen Adam's race, "the second death," of eternal woe,—all this falls infinitely short of the death of God's own Son as God's sentence against that which has wrought all ruin whether in earth or hell. Christ's death was a demonstration of God's abhorrence of sin.

One meaning of the word precious in the Hebrew is *weighty*, or of great moral value and force.

Death is the end of life, therefore weighty. There is no more work for the dead on earth; they are cut off from all below the skies.

I said, death is weighty because the end of life; I now say it is more weighty because it is at the end

of existence on earth, but hardly even a break in
real existence. Some who wrest the Scriptures to
their own destruction say death ends the existence
of the unsaved forever; there is no resurrection for
them. Jesus answers and confounds all these in his
narration of the rich man and Lazarus.

The death of the saints is weighty in impression
and influence:

First, on the unsaved. The triumphant death of
a saint is an argument which no man, however infidel or base, can controvert. We say to the wicked
man or infidel, "Your child died praising God," to
another, "Your wife," another, "Your father," or,
"Your mother; are you not glad?" Either will say,
"Yes," or turn away silent with a tear in the eye.
More than one unbeliever has been conquered by
the death of the saints.

Second, on the saved. "Our people die well,"
said Wesley. When I read the living testimony,
given for years, of Wesley to salvation, to entire
sanctification, and of his dying testimony to the
same, and the living and dying testimony of many
others; when I read of the multitude which no man
could number, who had washed their robes—washed
them not in heaven, but down here where the fountain for sin and uncleanness has been opened;—
when I know of all this I am mightily girded to en-

dure, and shout unto the end of the line of holiness, even that of entire sanctification.

No dying saint ever complained that the way was too holy, too self-denying, too separate from a vain, pleasure-loving, God-forgetting world.

How weighty, how precious are the last words of the saints! Hear Paul's words in the face of death, "Be not thou therefore ashamed of the testimony of our Lord, nor of me his prisoner: but be thou partaker of the afflictions of the gospel according to the power of God."—2 Tim. 1:8. "Precious in the sight of the Lord is the death of his saints."

The word precious in the Hebrew language has a variety of shades of meaning. One of these is that of *costly*. What did it cost God to secure such a death as that of the saint? All that it cost him to secure salvation for man. Paul tells it (1 Cor. 2:2): "For I determined not to know anything among you, save Jesus Christ"—

"Oh, yes, Paul, that is grand."

"Wait, wait," says he; "If I had to stop here I am lost and you and all are lost."

"Well, say it again, Paul; say it all."

Hear him, while the angels listen with eyes strained to look into the mystery, "I determined not to know anything among you, save Jesus Christ, and *him crucified.*"

Now hear that song over yonder, "Unto him that loved us and washed us"—in the river of life,—oh, no, no—"in *his own blood*, and hath made us kings and priests unto God and his Father; to him be glory and dominion forever and ever. Amen." But this last could never be only for the first.

Another signification of the word "precious" is, beautiful, splendid, glorious. The death of the saints is such *in assurance*. This assurance is most positive—a hope sure and steadfast. Hope is called "the swimming thought." This hope swims, is buoyed up on a stream of glory, and this stream flows into the ocean of Glory. Hope, assurance, swimming on the river of life; can this be death? "Dying, yet behold we live." He who died and rose for me says, "Whosoever liveth and believeth in me shall never die."—John 11:26.

The last moment is hastening on. The silver cord which binds to the shore of time is being loosened; the golden bowl which pours the red current of life is being broken. Friends are weeping, wringing their hands, hearts breaking. O my brother! O my sister! What is the prospect now? "All is well. Weep not for me." Then the dying one is the strong one, and consoles and sustains the rest.

The death of the saints is grand, glorious *in triumph*. There is a death at the entrance of every spiritual triumph. Death is weighty in a double sense, because while it ends existence on earth, it by no means ends all existence, but brings into a new phase of being. This may be illustrated by a river: first a spring, then a brook. It flows on, grows into a majestic stream on which great ships may ride. Now how still the waters become, how glassy. There! they plunge down the mighty falls. Is the river ended, lost? No; it is only purified, enlivened and made stronger, and flows on and on. Such is the stream of life. It leaps the falls of death, but only to flow on with deeper and wider meaning forever.

The death of the saints is precious—delightful. What! the death of the saints delightful to God? Yes, in a sense, because of the glory to follow. "Count it all joy when ye fall into divers temptations."—God must joy when we do. "Glory in tribulations also."—Then God must glory in our tribulations. The Lord glories, then, in a sense, in the trials and even in the death of his saints.

"*Precious*"; for now all peril is passed. Probation is over. No more "ifs" as conditions of getting to heaven. No more danger of falling and apostasy. No more temptations. No more devils and children of the devil. No more battles with possible defeat, but *eternal* salvation. Once through the door of death, and through the gate of pearl into the city golden, there forever. Every pain of body or spirit is precious to God. For a body diseased, subject to pain and death, will be given a glorified body; and what is that? "Who shall change our vile body, that it may be fashioned like unto his glorious body, according to the working whereby he is able even to subdue all things unto himself,"—this answers. For every pang of nature, and that even sanctified, at separation by death from loved friends, will be given the blessedness of eternal reunion and communion. For every groan here, a shout there; for each sigh of mourning an immortal song.

SERMON II.

"For the Lord God is a sun and shield."—Psa. 84:11.

THE sun is the great source of light and heat; some say the sole source. Some hold that all the heat in air, water, wood and coal comes from it; so that, in a sense, the sun boils our pots and drives our engines.

Being the great source of light and heat the sun is also the great source of vitality. A plant shut away from light will grow pale and die, and shut away from all heat as well as light death is soon and certain.

The Sun of righteousness is the grand and sole fountain of light and heat to the soul. "In him was life, and the life was the light of men." As plants grow sickly when withdrawn from the natural sun, so do the plants of our heavenly Father's planting when withdrawn from the Sun of righteousness.

208

Plants on the farther side of a well-lighted room
will not thrive like those right in the window. So
it is with spiritual plants. Therefore, instead of
shunning the light, let us crowd into it.

Plants in a room will lean towards and stretch out
after the light. Some flowers follow the sun. So
should we do.

But many do not love the light. "This is the
condemnation, that light is come into the world,
and men loved darkness rather than light, because
their deeds were evil." Many will not endure the
light. They run from it like owls, bats and raven-
ous beasts. Others hail it for a time, and rejoice in
it; but soon it shines on too narrow a way, it uncovers idols and crosses which were hidden before, and
they shrink from it; they turn into compromisers,
like bats flitting between daylight and dark.

The sun saves from blindness. Let a man be put
where no sounds can fall upon his ear and he becomes deaf; because the ear eats sound and without
it starves. So the eye eats light and without it
starves. Let us then open the eyes of our souls
wide to the light and drink it in.

The sun imparts strength, heals. Those are most
healthy who live in the sun.

The sun softens some things and hardens others.
The sun enlivens and nourishes some things and

dries up others. Here are two branches on the vine; the more the sun shines on one the more green and fruitful it grows, while the more he shines on the other the more dry and barren it grows. The one really grows in the vine; the other is really only stuck in.

The sun sweetens some things and sours others. He shines on a flower, and it not only grows more beautiful but more fragrant. He shines on an orange and ripens it into deliciousness. He shines on other things and they turn into rank sourness. The sourest of all things turned sour by the sun are those which once were alive but have become disconnected from the source of life, as fruit severed from the tree turning into vinegar. Such are many backsliders, especially those who still make a big profession.

The sun drives away fogs, damps and clouds. The fog shuts out the scene or makes every thing dim and indistinct. The sun shines. What a change! So spiritually.

The sun saves from fearful death.

The sun speaks with a still small voice. Who ever heard him make a noise? Who ever heard that mighty, glowing wheel creak or whirr? Yet look at his works. He shines on the waters—the ponds, rivers, creeks, lakes, seas and oceans—and lifts them into the firmament. How do the waters get to the highlands? They cannot run up hill; and if the streams ran down all the time without any supply for their upper fountains, they would run dry into the ocean, and then the great deep would rise above its bounds and overflow many islands and parts of continents. What prevents? The sun drawing the waters by evaporation from the oceans and making it run straight up hill. "They go up by the mountains; they go down by the valleys unto the place which thou hast founded for them."—Ps. 104: 8. So the sun runs our water wheels as well as our engines.

There are one hundred and forty-seven millions of square miles of ocean and sea, to say nothing of the expanse of lakes and rivers. The sun draws from this one hundred and forty-seven millions of square miles of ocean over one hundred billions of tons of water daily. Think, one hundred billion tons daily! This would fill a lake sixty miles square and twenty-four deep, or six hundred miles long, six miles wide and twenty-four feet deep. And yet in all this stupendous working how still! The sunbeam just kisses the face of the waters and woos upward the delicate mist, unseen as the air. It floats, floats, on thinner than gossamer wing, above the land, above the mountains, until oceans hang by slenderest, golden threads of sunlight above our heads. So works the Sun of righteousness. Even Christ in the flesh went about and put in motion the mighty interests of His kingdom, not with clashing armies and ostentatious senates, but how humbly, meekly and still! And God, "a Sun," the Holy Ghost—who ever heard him make a noise of himself? I never have, and yet who so mighty in his works?

Oh, I love "the still small voice." "Amen," says some velvet-eared formalist. Very well; but we go on to say: *the sun causes a commotion.* He shines with intensest heat on some particular portion of the atmosphere, expands and rarifies or makes it lighter, and the surrounding cooler air being heavier naturally flows in and displaces the warmer and lighter, just as water lifts and displaces oil. The result is air in motion, or wind. When the air is uncommonly heated in one locality and in another, not far off, is cool, it rushes in furiously displacing the hot air;—at the rate of twenty miles an hour, a furious wind; fifty, a tornado; one hundred, an awful hurricane. What is the cause of all this? The still small voice of the sun whispering to the air. There is another wind, the result of the action of the Sun of righteousness. See that company. They have been tarrying in that upper room some

ten days. Hark! what noise is that? A hurricane
is coming. "And suddenly there came a sound
from heaven as of a rushing mighty wind, and it
filled all the house where they were sitting." You
all know the result of that wind, and the accompanying fire. A mighty commotion was made.
Those blown upon were mocked by many as
drunken. That wind came through the operation
of the Sun of righteousness. Ezekiel tells of a
wonderful wind which blew dry bones together and
made them live.

The sun purifies. See that carrion. The sun
shines upon it and decomposes it, literally dries it
up,—that is, turns it into gases, which go up. The
sun makes himself very useful in this way. The
earth would soon become a mountain of filth without this ministration. Oh, what a servant we have
up yonder in the blue! He is a king, walking
through his limitless realm with thirty worlds hanging like gems upon his garments. One of these
worlds, our earth, swings around him in a modest
walk of only five hundred million miles a year;
while the star Herschel, eighteen hundred million
miles from the sun, circles around him in a path of
nine billion miles. And yet that king is a scavenger for us. So the Sun of righteousness purifies.
He is the scavenger to cleanse a world all befouled

with filth more abominable than any physical pollu-
tion; for the foulest carrion the sun ever looked
upon is innocent by the side of a dead soul up-
turned in the face of the Sun of righteousness,
bloated with the gases of pride, uncleanness and
enmity against God.   Yonder sun of nature sits
upon his golden throne and does the dirty work for
us; but the Sun of righteousness came down from
his throne, and became a servant to those who were
the slaves of the fiend.   If yonder sun should fall
from his place, and carry the spheres in mighty
ruin with him, it would not be so tremendous an
event as when the Sun of righteousness came down
to take up and bear away the uncleanness of a
world.

The sun in purifying often makes great disturbance. See those piles of offal in that city. The
sun shines upon them, poison fumes steam around
and a pestilence sweeps the nations. Is the sun to
blame? No; but those who allowed the filth to
gather. So the Sun of righteousness shines directly
and through his mediums upon communities and
churches steeped in worldliness and corruption. A
great disturbance ensues; hypocritical churches are
rent. "Think not that I am come to send peace on
earth: I came not to send peace, but a sword. For
I am come to set a man at variance against his

father, and the daughter against her mother, and the daughter-in-law against her mother-in-law. And a man's foes shall be they of his own household."— Matt. 10:34–36. Are the Sun of righteousness and his mediums to blame for this disturbance? No; but the heaps of filth shone upon, and those who allowed them to gather.

The sun not only purifies but he also makes beautiful. He is beautiful in himself. Millions have worshiped the sun. We do not wonder at it. Millions of Egyptians have bowed down to an ungainly bullock, and to toads and bugs. We would rather worship the sun any day, although the spirit of idolatry is equally manifest, whether in the worship of a bug, or a sun, or a bit of yellow metal, or a colored rag. The sun makes nature beautiful. The change from winter to spring comes through the sun. Every color of the landscape—of the green fields and woods—is caused by him. We have a lily in our garden. I sometimes sit and look at it, and look, thinking about a man who walked in Judæa eighteen hundred years ago and talked of lilies and Solomon, until my eyes grow moist. Who painted it? The sun. His beams were the pencils which, dipped in celestial hues, tinted the pearly white with colors fit to adorn an angel's wing. The Sun of righteousness makes beautiful. He is beau-

tiful in himself—"the one altogether lovely." I
worship this Sun. He makes the saints beautiful.
I used to know an old negro, crooked, poor, ragged.
I saw another man, handsome, what the world calls
fine appearing, with a little white patch in front of
him, called a lamb-skin, and a jeweled collar around
his neck. He was at the head of a great funeral
procession, with a splendid Bible slung before him.
He bore the grand title of high priest. His breath
was a compound of tobacco fumes, brandy and
lager beer; and his words at the grave kept on the
dodge to prevent the oaths, which were his accustomed talk, from slipping in. Some looked on and
called it, "beautiful." But old black John, who if he
had been seen alone in an African woods might
have been mistaken for a gorilla, and old Aunt
Nancy, with a face something like an Egyptian
mummy, her voice splitting all into quavers, semi-
quavers and demi-semi-quavers when she sang and
shouted,—these two old saints looked a thousand
times more beautiful to me than that Mason priest,
or than all the gods and goddesses of earthly
beauty. And why? Because the Sun shone upon
them, lighting up and making beautiful their souls
and faces. What makes a company of saints seem
so beautiful? "Why, you all look like angels," says
some one, his own face aglow. O, the Sun is shin-

ing on them; that is all. What made Stephen's
face glow right through the blood which streamed
from his bruised head and brow? The Sun. No
wonder that fourteen loads of saints were willing to
ride, some of them nearly a hundred miles, and in
lumber wagons, to attend our late Minnesota camp-
meeting. Why did these saints, many of them
tender women, go shouting along the way? They
were going to see a company whom the Sun shone
upon.

The sun is a symbol of benevolence. He shines
on those who can make him no return. He is free,
he shines alike upon all. The beggar can look up
equally with the grandee and say, "My sun." Thank
God! the sun can't be monopolized; for if he could
be some company of rich rascals would get him,
and we should have to buy sunshine as we do kero-
sene.

The sun is a symbol of stability. How old he is!
Six thousand years have gone; yet he is just as
young as when the morning stars sang together.
He formed one of that mighty choir, and not one
of his golden locks has turned grey. He looked
upon Eden. He saw father Adam and mother Eve.
He witnessed the first murder. He shone on
Methuselah when a puling babe, and also when he
passed away in his nine hundred and sixty-ninth

year. He saw Noah, and beamed aslant the deck
of the ark. His rays trembled over the burning
Sodom. He glimmered on the knife Abraham
raised to slay his son. He watched over Moses in
the bulrushes. He saw him take off his shoes before the burning bush. He saw the Nile run blood
and a million frogs leaping. He saw the children
of Israel in the wilderness. He kissed Moses' brow
when he died on Pisgah, and in his golden car was
the only one besides God and the angels who
attended his funeral. He saw the three Hebrew
boys walk out of the furnace. He saw the holy
child Jesus, and refused to look when he hung upon
the cross. He was riding high in his car when Paul
was on his journey to Damascus. He saw him with
the fury on his face, and then in a moment saw him
not; for a light shone around the slaughterer, so
much brighter than his own, that his burning eye
was dazzled into blindness. Soon he saw him
meekly led into the city. He shone upon his wondrous pilgrimages, and gleamed a parting smile to
him from the headsman's ax. He shone on all the
ancient saints. He saw the stakes, and beasts, and
cauldrons of boiling oil and other instruments
which sent sixty millions of martyrs out of great
tribulation to Mt. Zion. He saw the sturdy Luther
a boy at home with his father the miner. He saw

him as he burned the pope's bull at Wittemberg,—a sacrifice as acceptable as any Jewish. He saw Wesley flying like the the apocalyptic angel with the everlasting Gospel. He saw the early Methodists; and he sees the Methodists now. The same sun which looked at all these is looking upon us to-day. Look at him there. Adam looked on that sun, and Abraham and all the sainted multitudes gone before. Empires and nations, kindreds, peoples and tongues have come and gone; but he shines there still, walking by the same rule and minding the same things. What a rebuke to the wavering and oscillating!

But that sun shall go out. Not so the Sun of righteousness; he shall never go out. And another thing will outlast the sun: "The world passeth away, and the lust thereof," and the heavens will be rolled together, and stars fall and suns expire; "but he that doeth the will of God abideth forever."

Thick darkness would rule without the sun. So thick moral darkness without the Sun of righteousness: whatever light man would have of God and duty would be like the pale beam of the fixed stars in a moonless night. The heathen for exampie.

The sun shines on darkness. At the creation, when first set in the firmament, he shone on stygian gloom. Each morning he illuminated a world man-

tled in shades. The Sun of righteousness shines
on darkness. When Christ came, "Darkness covered the earth, and gross darkness the people."
Idolatry ruled; and those who did not bow to stocks
and stones were conceited philosophers, to whom
the gospel was foolishness and its Author a fool.
The Jewish church was a whited sepulchre. The
Scriptures say, "Darkness was upon the face of the
deep," an eternity old. What darkness! When the
command went forth, "Let there be light," what a
change! But what was that deep compared to that
other deep, the heart, and the darkness covering it?
and what that change compared to that when God
says, "Let there be light," and the Sun of righteousness arises, and that soul has its first day? This
change is well called, "Marvellous."

The sun uncovers works of darkness. Thieves
skulk when morning comes. The Sun of righteousness uncovers the works of the rulers of the darkness of this world, the wiles of the devil. Satan's
favorite way of working is in the dark, under a
cover of deception, which is lying. A lie belongs
to darkness, and will pass very well until the light
shines upon it. The Sun of righteousness reveals
the real character of persons to themselves and to
others. He uncovers the wickedness of churches.
He uncovers the "unfruitful works of darkness."

How Masonry hides from the Sun and resents any light thrown upon itself! How different the gospel, that invites examination! Its author instead of saying, "Shut it up in some distant, mystical cave of a lodge; and let not its ineffable light shine on any minors, cripples, beggars and women," says, "Go into all the world, and preach it to every creature, especially to the poor, rich in faith, whom God hath chosen." The hymn may be taken quite literally:

> " Hear him ye deaf; his praise, ye dumb,
>   Your loosened tongues employ;
> Ye blind, behold your Savior come;
>   And leap, ye lame for joy."

The sun shining on a world lying in darkness and sleep, awakens it to life and motion. Some day climb the mountain, and look down upon the slumbering world, the city, the country. Yonder graveyard is not more still. But see! there gleams the lower rim of sky. Now the east blushes as the bride about to meet the groom. See! there steps out the king, his radiant robes sweeping the earth and heavens. Now a world is alive. A thousand forests pour forth their music, a mighty organ; the lowing herds hail the opening day; and man from a thousand hills and vales, the city full and country wide, starts forth out of the womb of darkness and death, —a mighty new birth! What is the cause of all this?

Yonder sun. Who can doubt the possibility of a resurrection after such a scene?

SERMON III.

"And gave him [Christ] to be the head over all things to the church."—Eph. 1:22.

CHRIST was the Head over the Old Testament dispensation.

The Old Testament Scriptures speak all the way through of a kingdom which is to be established in the latter days, of which Christ is Head. The first intimation is given among the first words God spoke after the fall, when he told the serpent that the seed of the woman should bruise his head. A being from some other world looking upon this, witnesses the fall amidst the beauty of Eden, hears the curse and sighs, "What shall be done?" He hears the promise of the seed, and catches his breath as at a flash of light in awful darkness, sees Abel's sacrifice and Noah's, hears promises to Abraham, hears Jacob foretell Shiloh, witnesses the sac-

223

rifices. "What does it mean? Surely some great
One is prefigured who is coming." The idea is
more distinct when Moses says, "The Lord thy God
will raise up unto thee a Prophet from the midst of
thee, of thy brethren, like unto me; unto him ye
shall hearken."—Deut. 18:15. In the divine delinea-
tions of Isaiah he catches a shadowy, glorious
glimpse of a crown and gasps, "Wonderful!" Now
a shadow of a thorn crown in place of the golden,
and a "visage so marred more than any man."—
Gone! "What does it mean?" I hear stately step-
pings in Daniel;—he is coming. The vision deepens
in Zechariah and Malachi. Now I catch wondrous
glimpses through the veil of a form and features ineffable. Who is it? Who has come marching
through the ages, down the path of four thousand
years? Then the veil bursts; the King is revealed;
and an anthem rolls like thunder from Bethlehem's
plain, "Glory to God in the highest, and on earth
peace, good will toward men."

It is an unspeakable dignity to be the one object
in whom such a book as the Bible heads. But this
Bible is not only *the* book, and the Book of God; it
is also the book of the Church, Zion's book. It is
her history; the history of her origin and foundation, and of her future prophetically. It is her code
of laws, her statute book, her manual of instruction,

her guide, her solace and her joy. And it is Zion's book in a double sense, and by a double right, because it is her Lord's, and she can say, "I am my Lords; and he is mine, with all he has."

On this canvas of Revelation, on this master painting hung in the galleries of time and eternity, one portrait stands out in the foreground—all else in the background—and that is Jesus. No, there is one thing more which stands with him in the foreground, by his side, and that is his Bride, his Wife. To this Christ the Father says, "Thy throne, O God, is forever and ever,"—that is, "Thou art King, Head." And he is Head over all things to, or for, the Church, for the saints collectively, and as the whole includes the part, for the saints individually. Are you a saint? You say, "I profess to be." Well, then, you have a Head, even Christ. Let us see if you have.

A man is dead without a head. Let a man get separated from his head, and there is not much life in him. This is so socially, politically and in military affairs. Any association, government or army without a head amounts to little. So a church, ecclesiastically, must have a head—those who have the rule. But a church may have a head ecclesiastical, and not spiritual, and be dead.

We must have a spiritual Head, even Christ.

With him as Head the individual, the Church has
life. What is life? Power over death physical;
over death spiritual; over the flesh, dead in sin;
over the carnal mind, which is death; over the
world, a collection of carnal minds; over the old
Adam—out of Romans seventh; over the devil, who
has the power of death.

The man knows as, or what his head knows.
Would you know spiritual and heavenly things? "let
that mind be in you which is in Christ Jesus," be
united to the Head. What a knowledge this will
bring in things divine! Some ignoramus in worldly
knowledge out-knows, out-talks, out-lives the most
of D. D's. Why? Because he's got a Head on him
now.

The man feels as the head feels. Our Head hates
sin, loves holiness, is full of love, peace and joy.
Why did David dance before the ark? Because he
was joined to the Head.

The man goes where his head goes. Christians
do not go into carnal amusements, though carried
on in the name of the Lord. The Head went into
the temple, and found the brethren buying and selling in the name of God, for religious purposes. He
whipped them out. So does the man or church who
has the Head. The great Head does not go into a
Free Mason lodge. He is by intrinsic Masonic law

left outside in the cold to suit Jews, Turks, Hindoos and deists who discard Christ. He is left out of all authorized Masonic rituals, out of all their scripture readings, out of the lodge prayers. What a Bible, without Christ! what a prayer, without Christ, "the only name under heaven, given among men, whereby we must be saved!" Now, no Christian goes inside such a place, when he knows of this crowding out of Christ; for no Christian can go where his Head does not go.

But we must say a word more on the text, "Head over all things to," or for, "the church." The Church means the redeemed; therefore Jesus is Head of all for the redeemed, and the Scriptures show that he is Head by virtue of his being Redeemer. He is Creator and Governor, not as God simply, but as the Redeemer of men. Col. 1:14 shows this, "In whom"—Christ—"we"—the saints or church—"have redemption." Redemption for the Church is the text of this wonderful sermon. Then it goes on, "who is the image of the invisible God,"—in Hebrews, "the express image of his person," very God then,—"the first born of every creature," man then. Here we have God-man, the Redeemer. Now it reads on, "for by him"—God-man, Redeemer—"were all things created." Why? Because he is God simply? No; for the Father

and Spirit are equally God. Why, then? Because
he is God-man. Why was Jesus Christ God-man, or
God manifest in the flesh? That he might be Redeemer is the prime and grand answer. And why
is this Redeemer called here pre-eminently the
Creator? Because by virtue of being Redeemer he
is Head over all things for the church, or Redeemed,
and to be this Head in the fullest sense he must be
Creator and Governor of all things.

Do you take in this mighty thought, that Jesus
Christ is Creator and upholder of the universe because he is Redeemer, and as Redeemer Head over
all things to the Church? So all creation relates to
redemption; and redemption relates to the redeemed or Church; therefore all creation relates to,
or is for, the Church. Now, let us read again Col.
1: 14–18: "In whom we have redemption: * * *
Who is the image of the invisible God, the first born
of every creature; for by him"—God-man, Redeemer—"were all things created, that are in heaven,"—
or in the heavens, all the worlds above us,—"and
that are in earth, visible and invisible, whether they
be thrones, or domions, or principalities, or powers:
all things were created by him and for him"—as
Redeemer, and for the redeemed,—"and he is before
all things, and by him all things consist." Now,
see how all this creating, and upholding, and govern-

ing culminates in the Church: "and he is the head of the body, the church: who is the beginning, the first born from the dead;"—that is, who died and rose again,—"that in all things he,"—as the one who died and rose, or who became Redeemer, for he did so solely to become Redeemer,—"that in all things he might have the pre-eminence"—or heading, and that heading for the Church.

We need not think it a thing incredible that the universe is made in reference to redemption, and for the redeemed; for a million universes all made for this would not equal the gift of God to man in Christ. "God so loved the world that he gave his only begotten Son," in whom potentially, the universe resides. The Son also gave himself,—"Even as Christ loved the church and *gave himself for her*" —gave himself to this one end, put all his being into it as his sole work. Now for the Maker of the universe to give himself was more than to give the universe, because the Maker is greater than the thing he makes.

The problem of the ages, yea, of time and eternity, is, How can God be just and yet the justifier of sinners? This problem is solved on this earth in redemption; and all intelligences, all worlds of intelligencies, are to learn from redemption the most glorious attributes of Jehovah, —his wisdom, in designing the scheme; his omnipotence, in carrying it through; his justice and abhorrence of sin, by sparing not the sinner's Substitute on Calvary; his mercy and his love.

Such a story as redemption cannot be, will not be, shut up in this little world. The angels know of it, and desire above all things to look into it. Devil's know it and cry, "We know thee who thou art, Jesus of Nazareth, the holy one of God." And if there are intelligencies, dominions, principalities and powers in the other stars, they know it, or will. Redemption is too big a thing, and too good, to keep in this nook, this crevice, of the creation; it is for the universe to know and endorse. The entire universe from center to circumference is related to redemption,—it is blood sprinkled, so to speak. From the worm that crawls, up to the last great sun which moves around the throne as its centre, with all suns and stars hanging as gems on its mantle of splendor; up to the seraphim who cry around the throne, "Holy, holy, holy, is the Lord of hosts; the whole earth is full of his glory,"—all exists because of redemption and the redeemed.

If false to this redemption, all things in the judgment will witness against me; and when the Redeemer—then Judge—says, "Depart from me ye cursed," the universe with one mighty voice will say, "AMEN." "How shall we escape, if we neglect so great salvation?"

It would seem extravagant to say that God exists for the Church; but so far as the Scriptures show he has, from all eternity, had his mind on her, and been shaping all things in reference to her, as Paul says—Eph. 3:11,—"According to the eternal purpose which he purposed in Christ Jesus our Lord." The old catechism asks, "What is the chief end of man?" and answers, "To glorify God, and enjoy him forever." We ask, "What is the chief end of God?" and answer reverently, but in the clear light of the Word, "To glorify man, and enjoy him forever." We need not stagger at this astounding doctrine through unbelief, because it is so great in behalf of man. Thousands stagger, to their eternal undoing, at the doctrine of a full and a present salvation from sin; because they think it too great and glorious for man to experience. We need not stagger, I say, when we consider Phil. 2:5-10 inclusive, a portion of which reads: "Who, being in the form of God,"—or, who being God—"thought it not robbery to be equal with God:"—or, as the New Version more correctly has it, "counted it not a prize to be on an equality with God, but emptied himself, taking the form of a servant." What words! as though Jesus was so taken up with redeeming man that he counted as more to be prized than even to be God to empty himself of divinity and become a man; and lower still, to become a servant; and lower still, to become obedient unto death; and lower still, even the death of the cross. Oh, my Lord and my God! what shall we say, what shall we do in the face of such unutterable condescension! As we try to take in these stupendous truths, all we can say to them is, "Herein is love," "even as Christ loved the church."

The Church—Zion—is the Lamb's wife. The scriptural idea is that a man is to love his wife better than anything else next to God; and we may truly say this is most positively the scriptural idea of the love of Christ for the Church. It may be said that a man may love his kindred, or friends, or children better than he does his wife. Well, Christ's wife is represented in the scriptures as embodying all kinds of precious relationships.— "And he stretched forth his hand towards his disciples"—his wife—"and said, Behold, my mother and my brethren." He said to her at one time, "Children, have ye any meat?" All endearing terms are used to show his love for his Church; but spouse, bride, wife with him embraces them all.

Christ has but one wife. Christ will never have any other wife but Zion. Jacob worked fourteen years to get his wife. Christ left the courts of glory for thirty-three years, and came into the world and worked most mightily, and died to get his wife. He had to die in order to this, and he will die but once the Bible says. And he liveth forevermore, and she will never die. Therefore, Zion will never have any other husband, and Christ will never have any other wife. And as he is the Honorable One of all the universe, the Head, and loves his wife the best of all, and seats her upon the throne by his side,—therefore, there can be no class of beings in any other world now or ever as exalted in the divine affections and regard as Zion. And what will the end of all this be: Rev. 21: 9,— "Come hither, I will show thee the bride, the Lamb's wife," said one of the seven angels to John. "And he carried me away in the Spirit to a great and high mountain, and shewed me,"—what? Why, the Lamb's wife. But it says, "and shewed me that great city, the holy Jerusalem, descending out of heaven from God." What does this mean? Is this the bride? It must be. But this is a city most glorious, Jerusalem the holy. Well, Zion, the Church, is called Jerusalem, sometimes. Has the Lord, so transported with the beauty of his bride, and ravished with love for her, lost his senses for a time, and is he showing a city in her stead by mistake? No, that cannot be, for he makes no blunders. And it goes on to say, "having the glory of God: and her light"—*her*, the bride's—"was like unto a stone most precious, even like a jasper stone, clear as crystal." Then he goes on to describe the city Jerusalem, the holy. What does it mean? It means, at least, that the Lamb's wife, the Church triumphant, is as beautiful and glorious as the city of God; that God himself can illustrate her beauty to man only by a picture of the city which, after all, is only a type, a parable, of her matchless loveliness, and which is to be her home and God's home forever.

SERMON IV.

FREEDOM.

"And ye shall know the truth, and the truth shall make you free."
"If the Son therefore shall make you free, ye shall be free indeed."—
John 8: 32, 36.

TRUTH includes all the laws and principles, moral and physical, according to which God has made and runs the universe with everything in it.

There can be no true and lasting freedom in anything without the truth, whether that thing be mental, moral, social, political, commercial, or even material and mechanical. The thing must work according to the laws or truth upon which God has based it, or it will be out of order and work ill. Men may conduct business fraudulently, and spread themselves like a green bay tree; but fraud in an individual, a corporation, or a state is a fowl which is sure to come home to roost in that green bay tree, and by its hideous croakings to advertise it to

the world and by its vile droppings to blast it. The
founders of the United States government to preserve freedom for the whites thought they must
keep the chains of American slavery on the blacks.
The most vengeful, fratricidal war the world has
ever seen; billions of dollars wasted, enough, as
Senator Stephens counts, to have bought every
slave of the four millions at five thousand dollars
apiece; one million of white men slain, a hundred
thousand of them starved and rotted in military
prison hells,—all this says, "There can be no real
and lasting freedom in government and politics
only as man keeps step with truth."

In religion the most ruinous bondage holds without the truth. A false religion is the biggest of
lies—the truth turned into a lie; and the more of
truth in it, we mean truth perverted, the more
deceptive and deadly. But above all beings bound
by chains of truth turned into a lie, the worldly,
orthodox-church professor is the most deluded.
Who was the most deluded man in Christ's day?
The Jew. Why? Because he was fatally wrong
and blind to it. There was much truth in his religion, but we know he turned it into a lie; and this
truth so perverted only made his delusion the
stronger. The light that was in him was darkness,
and how great that darkness! So Jesus pronounced

him a slave. He was in deeper and more ruinous
bondage than the heathen. According to this principle, the most deluded of all beings is the man
under the gospel who professes faith in Christ,
while in Spirit and works denying him; and the
nearer he comes to Christ and the cross without
really touching them, and rests in a faith that he
does touch them, the deeper his delusion and bondage. The Jews rested in a faith in Abraham as
their father, through whom they were heirs of the
covenant. But Jesus in the context of my texts
pronounces their faith not real; for says he, "If ye
were Abraham's children [the children of true faith
in him], ye would do the works of Abraham." So
the worldly professor now professes faith in Jesus
Christ,—"Oh, Jesus is my Saviour"; while Jesus
answers, "Why call ye me, Lord, Lord, and do not
the things I command you?" The faith of the Jew
in Abraham comforted him, and made him at times
ecstatic; but it was a false comfort and ecstacy,
which only made stronger the chains of delusion
and bondage. And so the faith of the world-
conformed professor now, makes him comfortable
and ecstatic it may be; but that only proves it the
more false and ruinous.

Christ told the Jews that only two things could
make them free: first, "And ye shall know the

truth, and the truth shall make you free"; and next, "If the Son therefore shall make you free, ye shall be free indeed." You notice he puts the truth before the Son; and how proper! for the soul must first be plied with truth before it is ready for the Son. Conviction of sin comes through the application of the truth to the conscience by the Holy Ghost; and when conviction is thus secured then is the time to cry, "Behold the Lamb of God, which taketh away the sin of the world."

We may say that before God made the universe he had a draught or model of the whole in his mind; and this was in all its parts truth, or many truths, moral and material. Whatever thing accords with this, and particularly as pertaining to the laws of its own being, is free; but if it does not so accord it is out of order, and trammeled or bound—not free, whether it be a machine, a worm, a man, or an angel. Adam before the fall was the model man, perfectly conformed to the divine draught, or truth, and consequently was free, gloriously free. But the moment he fell out of line with truth he fell into sin and bondage.

The great work of Deity ever since has been to bring man back to the model—to make him free. This is the burden of the Atonement,—to secure a soul pure and holy here, and at last a soul and body glorified, perfectly reflecting truth. The most tremendous battle the universe has ever known, or ever will know, was fought for this. The battle-ground was on this earth. In the battle of Water-loo one spot was contested for by both armies as the key of the battle,—the Chateau of Hougou-mont; that lost all was lost, that gained all was gained. So in this battle one spot was the key, and that was Calvary. The grand efforts of the cap-tains on either side were to gain this. Satan used all his powers to keep Jesus from Calvary, and to gain it. He knew the meaning of, "It shall bruise thy head." He had read Isaiah 53. He tried on the mount of temptation to keep Jesus from the commanding point. He tried to get him killed before the time. But Jesus contended for the position. He said, "I *must go* unto Jerusalem, and suffer many things of the elders and chief priests and scribes, and be killed, and be raised again the third day."—Matt. 16:21. In Gethsemane he "offered up prayers and supplications with strong crying and tears unto him that was able to save him from death, and was heard in that he feared."—Heb. 5:7. When Satan saw that the Son, the seed of the woman, would gain the position—Calvary, he seems to have uncorked the vials of his wrath and said: "Well, if you will die, you shall. Now, men,

make it as hard as you can. Let all classes unite,—
the ecclesiastical in the great Jewish Church, the
civil in the great Roman Empire, the military in the
soldiers. Let the death be the worst in the world,
the most cruel, the most base and infamous. For
three hours let men mock him, let priests and the
mob cry, 'Aha, aha.' Now three hours for devils
and the heart-crushing burden." They come; and
so thick are the legions of the pit that the sun is
hidden. "Now, while in the midnight of the hour
of the power of darkness, see his feet tread the
wine-press of iron spikes. While his heart is
breaking, fiends flap your vampire wings in
his face." See!—I seem to see the old serpent
himself coming on. He rolls his black snake
folds out of the iron gate of hell. See! he glides
up Calvary. He looks at the cross. He mounts
it. He winds around the quivering body. There
he looks Jesus in the eye, thrusts his forked tongue
of fire in his face, and hisses, "Aha, is this the
way thou art bruising the serpent's head? Now
I'll bruise thy heel." He draws back his head.
See! he unfolds his fangs that have poisoned the
whole of Adam's race and filled hell. There! he
strikes them deep into Jesus' heart. Pierced with
the mortal pain the Saviour cries, "Eloi, Eloi, lama
sabachthani?"—"My God, my God, why hast thou

forsaken me?" His heart breaks. The sins of the whole world, in a sense, run out with its blood, washed away. The Son cries with a loud voice, "It is finished." The earth quakes. The temple veil rends. Satan drops like lightning, dead, *dead*, so far as hunting Christ's saints is concerned; for through death Christ destroyed "him that had the power of death, that is, the devil."—Heb. 2:14.

Poor slave you are free. There is your emancipation paper on the cross. We read, "In whom we have redemption through his blood, the forgiveness of sins, according to the riches of his grace."—Eph. 1:7.

Now the Son makes free by making square with the truth. Are you square with this? If not, I exhort you in the name of God to get so. Get in line with truth, with Jehovah the God of truth, or you will be crushed at last. If a man is on a train of cars and there is no possibility of running off the track, he is safe no matter how fast it runs; but let him get out of order with that train, let him get in its way, and afoul of that locomotive, and he will fare badly, will be crushed. So if you are in line with truth, with God's order, you are safe going on the lightning express to the depot of the New Jerusalem; but if you are out of gear with that train, and in the way of that engine, woe unto you.

All the disorder in the universe, anywhere and everywhere, comes because devils and men pile obstructions on the track, and the engine and train of Truth and Providence—which is the Son working out the truth—are obliged to plow their way through these devils and men and their evil inventions. This train makes terrible work, leaving in its wake a host of fallen angels broken and howling, with nations and individuals crushed and mangled. These will be crowded by it at last into hell. And then it will run on forever, over the plains and through the vales and along the mountain sides of Glory, and all on board send up everlasting hallelujahs.

When slaves are freed they retain their nature and habits. But the mighty Son introduces into a further freedom by transforming the slave nature. He conforms the heart to the truth by the power of the Holy Ghost who is procured by him. The Holy Ghost regenerates and then sanctifies the slave nature. He writes the law on the heart in letters of burning love. Are you not afraid of the law, of its lightnings and thunders? No; for the law is now on my side, or rather I am on the side of the law, or truth. When I was a rebel, I trembled because the great guns of the law were firing on me in the enemies' ranks; but since I have gone

over to the side of the law, the guns are all for me
and only against my enemies. No devil can touch
me; for as soon as one tries, the guns are turned on
him and he is blown to pieces. I lie down and go
to sleep right under the muzzles of the artillery of
Omnipotence; and sleep sweetly too, for I sleep the
sleep of the just, or of one in agreement with eternal truth.

Oh, it is blessed to be free, free in life and free in
death! When men come to die tremendous considerations move them. At the time the steamers
Narragansett and Stonington collided what a
prayer-meeting was held by the men, women and
children perishing in the water! The wail was
heard far and near, "O God, have mercy on me!
Save my wife! Save my children!" And if Tyn-
dall had been there very likely he would have
forgotten his sneering prayer test and prayed too.
Now the sting of death is sin; and "sin is the
transgression of the law" or truth. But if I have
through obedience of the truth honored the law,
then I am free from sin and death has lost its
sting. So the redeemed girt about with truth go
down to the grave shouting, "O death, where is
thy sting?" And in the resurrection morn, in the
power of the Son who says, "I am the resurrection
and the life," they will spring out of the grave

shouting, "O grave, where is thy victory?" Oh, to be free in regard to the judgment! Judgment day means law day. If I am square with the law—the truth—what hurt can the judgment do me?

And then to be free in regard to eternity,—free to think of it with holy joy and free when we get there! The Roman Empire under Augustus Cæsar filled the world. A criminal found no place to hide himself; the emperor could lay his hand on him anywhere, for he owned the world civilly. Where then in eternity will the moral criminal find a place to escape from the Emperor of the Universe? Let him look here or there he must cry, "Whither shall I go from thy Spirit? or whither shall I flee from thy presence?"—Psa. 139:7. But a loyal citizen of the Roman Empire, with the emperor's passport, was safe anywhere, and free. So will it be with the redeemed in eternity; with the passport stamped with the seal royal of the Son—Immanuel—they can range the universe.

SERMON V.

"PROPHESY UNTO THE WIND."

"Then said he unto me, Prophesy unto the wind, prophesy son of man, and say to the wind, Thus saith the Lord God; Come from the four winds, O breath, and breathe upon these slain, that they may live."—Ezek. 37:9.

THE LORD here counseled Ezekiel to invoke the Holy Spirit to breathe upon the bodies lying before him. Wind symbolizes the Spirit.

Wind purifies. It is one of the great purifying agents in nature. On a hot day, when poisonous gases are steaming all around, and life seems a burden, how grateful to have the breeze or wind spring up! It sweeps away the gases; and the tired laborer lifts his hat from his brow and says, "Oh, how good!" The vast ocean of atmosphere would become a stagnant expanse of pestilence and death were there no wind.

The Wind of Heaven is the great purifier of the

moral atmosphere. Were it not for the Holy Spirit, what would be the condition of mankind! There would be no Bible, and no restraint on the sinful heart, and earth would soon present a scene similar to hell. What a change is wrought in persons and communities by this purifying Wind! Profanity is blown away, and praise brought instead. The fumes of rum and of tobacco are blown away; cards are blown away; evil tempers are chased off, and tempers sweet as the breath of heaven wafted through each heart and house.

Wind, or air, is one of the essentials of life. Speedy death ensues without it. People die for want of breath, or air—that is, air in motion; in other words, for want of wind; for every breath is a miniature wind. And so spiritually, men are dying for want of the Wind of Heaven. They lie abject and groveling, hidden behind their idols, down on "the plain" of worldliness, on the lowlands, amidst the marshes and bogs and malaria. They have not escaped for their lives to the Mountain—to Mount Zion, where the Wind has free scope.

The Wind Ezekiel prophesied to had remarkable life-giving properties. Witness the scene,—bones, dry bones, a valley full, "and, lo, they were *very* dry." He worked, and preached, and got them together, and sinews upon them, and flesh. He had got up quite a respectable congregation and church, and there was a great shaking among them—powerful conviction under his prophesying, or preaching; but they had no life. Now God says, "Prophesy unto the wind." He did, and said, "Thus saith the Lord God, Come from the four winds, O breath, and breathe upon these slain, that they may live. So I prophesied as he commanded me, and the breath came into them, and they lived."

Wind is necessary for fire, as seen in the draught of a furnace. And it is not the draught simply which makes the fire burn, but the gases or elements of fire in the draught. A draught of air, loaded with certain kinds of gases, will extinguish fire, and life also—as seen in the gas thrown by the fire-exterminator engine. Pure wind is full of elements of fire. The Wind of Heaven is necessary to kindle the Divine Fire in the soul. That Wind is full of "the Holy Ghost and fire." On Pentecost, along with the Wind, came "cloven tongues like as of fire." David says, "While I was musing the fire burned." The Wind breathed upon him.

Wind is sometimes strong. On the day of Pentecost, it came, "a sound from heaven as of a mighty rushing wind, and it filled all the house where they were sitting." The effect on the saints was, that "they were all filled with the Holy Ghost," and inspired to speak some sixteen different languages, telling the wonderful works of God. It set Peter, the coward and denier, to preaching with uncompromising boldness; and breathed them all full of courage for Jesus. The effect on sinners was, that three thousand were blown that day clear from the Babylon of captivity to sin and Satan, to the Jerusalem of salvation.

"The Wind" sometimes blows down tall and strong trees, such as are spoken of in Isaiah 2:13: "the cedars of Lebanon that are high and lifted up, and the oaks of Bashan,"—Saul of Tarsus, for example, laid flat in the dust. It blows away sandy foundations,—"and the winds blew and beat upon that house, and it fell." It blows away false hopes. It blows off cloaks. What a commotion a good, strong gust from the land of holiness and power and glory will make among those "having a form of godliness but denying the power thereof"! their foundations blown away, every rag of a hope in tatters, and "the dear church," made up mostly of lumber from the forests of "the plain," shaking and racking in every timber. Amen, Lord. "The Wind" has blown one great church to pieces—the Jewish—because they compromised and trimmed with the world; and others may profit by their example.

Wind, when blowing a hurricane, sometimes blows up grass, and weeds, and flowers by the roots—literally tearing up the ground. It makes bad work with the flower-beds. So the Wind of Heaven sometimes blows over the flower-bed, the carnal heart, and makes bad work with the flowers growing there.—What kind of flowers? Rag flowers. The only soil in the world that will produce a rag flower is the carnal heart. Clay, loam, prairie, muck, or even a dung-hill, cannot be made to grow a rag flower; but the carnal heart has produced acres of them. They root in the heart, and commonly sprout out at the head. We have known this Wind to blow a good many of them right out by the roots. It is so penetrating, it goes right to the roots of things; and brings along with it seeds from heaven, and drops them in the torn furrows, when they spring up and bloom in divine loveliness.

The wind, blowing a hurricane, sometimes seizes fowls and blows the feathers out of them, nearly as clean as if they had been picked. So we have known this Wind to seize some human gay birds, and pluck them of plumes and feathers and streamers.

A little obstruction may prevent a draught of air from blowing, which may be necessary to very important results,—as the small damper to a large stove. Shut

it, and the fire goes out; open, and a great flame
blazes. So it is with the fire in the soul. A small
duty neglected, a little cross rejected, will shut off
the Wind of Heaven, and the heart becomes cold
and finally frozen. One person may be as a damper
to a whole meeting. By refusing to yield to the
Spirit, he shuts off the flow, and all are frigid, or
burdened and distressed. By obeying, the Wind
flows in, the fire blazes, and all are warmed. One
person once shut the Wind of Heaven from the
whole Israelitish nation—three millions of men,
women and children—and caused them to be the
sport of evil winds. His name was Achan. A
wedge of gold and a Babylonish garment stuffed
into his heart shut off the Wind from him, and he
from the whole nation. Let us learn.

Let us notice some of the things which prevent
the Wind from blowing upon the soul:

Some idol, standing between the soul and the
Spirit. It may be very small; but it is no smaller
than the person or soul making it an idol. The
size of the soul morally can be measured by the
size of the idol; and as all idols are really little and
mean compared with God, how little is every sinful,
worldly soul, and it can hide behind how small a
thing! Some bauble, some mean dishonesty, some
worldly honor—infinitely paltry in its largest meas-

ure compared with "the honor which cometh from
God only"—keeps the Wind of Heaven from blowing upon it. Some—alas! we have reason to believe many—get a great church between them and
the Wind. They reason, "It has a glorious past."
But what is its present? "It is mighty; it has
millions of members, and great divines, and countless money, and powerful influence." So much the
worse, if it denies the power of godliness, and
stands as an idol between you and God. Oh, be-
ware of this church idolatry! Feel through all
forces and externals for the truth,—and that alone
will not answer; for "the letter without the Spirit
killeth." Does the Wind have free scope upon and
through it? If not, it is no better than Ezekiel's
valley of men perfect in form—in bodies of bone,
covered with muscle and sinews—but having no life
in them. Some lurk behind a wall of prejudice, and
some behind a screen of starch—the starch of self-
dignity and false education in spiritual things, and
of unbelief. They feel the Wind coming, and fear
that if they give it anything of a chance, they will
be blown out of balance in some way, and up goes
the screen and they dodge behind.

*Various ways are resorted to by churches to "raise the
wind,"*—as festivals, fairs, and shallow revivals, and
other worldly contrivances. None will be truly

convicted and saved, unless the Wind of Heaven is raised. And this can be done only by removing the obstacles, leveling the idols, and humbling ourselves in the dust. Then it will have free scope, and all earth and hell cannot keep it from blowing.

Wind stirs up the great ocean. This is necessary to keep its waters pure and lively. So the Wind of Heaven often blows on that great deep, the human heart, and stirs it to the very bottom. Nothing but this can stir the soul to its nethermost depths. Persons may think that they are as intensely excited as possible by some temporal event, and influence, but they know nothing of the intensity of feeling the heart is susceptible of, until the Wind of Heaven stirs it. What sorrow like that when this Wind blows on the dark waters of the sinful spirit, and stirs up emotions like these: "I have sinned against God; I have rebelled against my heavenly Father; I have crucified my Savior; I have grieved the Holy Comforter." What groans like these? And what joy like that when this same Wind blows on these waters, regenerating and purifying them!

The ocean is in motion all the time, through the tides and various agencies; but still it needs wind to stir it and keep it pure,—*and not mere common wind, but every now and then a gale and a hurricane.* So does the deep of the human heart need not only the common influences of the Spirit, but every now and then a gale—a hurricane—stirring up from the very bottom and setting all in motion.

O Wind! breathe, breathe a hurricane! And as the great waves roll and roar around the Rock of Ages, and on the golden beach of salvation, every roar shall be, Glory! Glory! Glory!

SERMON VI.

LITTLE THINGS.

THE Bible furnishes numerous instances of the importance of little things. But the act on which hung the most stupendous issues, was an offense, seemingly, the smallest possible: that was, eating a little fruit. The Lord told Adam and Eve that they could eat of the fruit of every tree but one, and in the day they ate thereof, they should surely die.

This must have been a literal eating; for if the fruit and eating were an allegory, as some say, then we may make the garden an allegory, and the man and woman an allegory; and then their descendants are an allegory. How little the act; how tremendous the consequences!—thrusting from the garden —a cursed earth—sweat and toil—and, worse than all, sin, sin! the foulest monster, the offspring of devils and fallen man. Look at the world now;

think of the daily wickedness, the discontent, the selfishness, intemperance, lust, prisons, murders. Think of the mighty wars, an earth drenched with blood. Think of the deaths. Think of these for one day,—*seventy thousand;* think of seventy thousand corpses; think of the funeral processions for one day. Think of all this, and then multiply by thousands of years, and how the mind recoils from the fearful aggregate. And when we reflect,

" 'Tis not the whole of death to die,"

and the mind pierces the veil and hears the wailing, and then sees the multitude, like a vast, black, ceaseless tide, rolling, hurrying on to that hell (and so it has been for sixty centuries), then we can form a little idea of the importance of one little act; for all was suspended on the eating of that fruit. How impressively this teaches that any transgression, no matter how apparently trivial, is awful!

The Bible teaches the importance of little things, when it speaks of "the little foxes which spoil the vines"; and more forcibly when it says, "For whosoever shall keep the whole law, and yet offend in one point, he is guilty of all." A point, in mathematics, means that which occupies no space; in morals, we may say, it is the smallest thing possible. How small then, seemingly, a point of the law,

And how important that little point, the infraction of which virtually constitutes a violation of the whole mighty law!—that law, the authority of which compasses the universe of intelligences, and to which the tallest archangel in reverential submission bows.

One sign of the importance of some little things pertaining to religion, is the opposition they meet with from the world and worldly churches. For instance, the little matter of apparel.—How any strictures on this are sneered at by the people of the world, and, alas! also, with but few exceptions, by ministers and church members. "What little business" is echoed from every side, "meddling with so little a matter as dress!" We might reply, that Paul meddled quite seriously with the little matter of the mode in which women should wear their hair. Now this contempt poured on this little thing of contending for plain attire, to the exclusion of all jewelry and artificial flowers, and costly array, is a proof, to our minds, of its importance. Why are they so excited about it, if so unimportant? Why such sneering and ridicule, and finally hatred and persecution, when urged to the practice of the plain Scripture injunction, "In like manner, also, that women adorn themselves in modest apparel, with shamefacedness and sobriety, not with broidered hair, or gold, or pearls, or costly array"? If so unimportant, as they aver, why not yield it as such, and be on the sure side—the side which is certainly safe—that of denial, and in accordance with the plain reading of the Scripture? This matter is little in itself; and yet, little as it is, nothing has a stronger hold on the mass of church members; and an enforcement of the simple word of God in this respect, as once enforced by the discipline of the Methodist Episcopal Church, would raise a commotion of the first magnitude. and would actually break up many of the magnificent establishments of the day.

Our littleness is shown by our hanging so on little things. And still, little as they are, we never could overcome them in our own strength; they are larger than we are; they master us, unless we have help from a foreign power—even God. Oh, how little we are!

Judas sold his Lord for thirty pieces of silver. How pitiable a sum—the price of a common slave—for the Son of God! How mean, how contemptible, the covetous, traitor spirit, which could do this! But thousands are selling their Lord for a smaller sum than thirty pieces of silver,—for some paltry bauble of pride. Think of it! the Lord of glory, a kingdom, a crown—all heaven—sold for a bit of jewelry. a piece of ribbon, a painted rag!

It is the policy of Satan, to make little things, connected with the service of God, seem unimportant; for in these often are involved great principles. He doubtless exults more over victories gained by little means, than by great. And the smaller and meaner the things by which he can accomplish so stupendous a work as the ruin of a soul, the greater his exultation. And we have thought, that he chuckles in diabolical jubilee to see ministers and churches often chasing after what they think to be lions, while "the little foxes," all unnoticed, are spoiling the vines. And what is worse, they, meanwhile, sneering at those who count the little foxes of sufficient consequence to call for a share of attention. How the following items of the divine statutes are violated: "Love not the world, neither the things that are in the world; for if any man love the world, the love of the Father is not in him." "For all that is in the world, the lust of the flesh, and the lust of the eyes, and the pride of life, is not of the Father, but is of the world." How this cuts off all unhallowed gratification of the passions and the palate, "all filthiness of the flesh and spirit"! How it puts its veto on all displays of vanity and pride in dress, equipage and building! How it applies its withering censure to the universal trimming for honor from men! "How can ye

believe who receive honor one of another, and seek
not the honor that cometh from God only?" "Ye
adulterers and adulteresses, know ye not that the
friendship of the world is enmity against God?"
Never was Satan so wheedling this world—this
great, big bulk of formalism and conceit called
Christendom—down to hell, by the mean, contemptible things of pride and earthly honor, as now.

The principles involved give importance to little things.
They are often signs or expressions of principles
which underlie the whole government of God,—
principles which must be respected, or disaster and
ruin will come upon the transgressors, and finally
ruin upon the entire divine government. Little
things, we repeat—little words and acts—are often
signs or expressions of great principles; as "the still
small voice" of God, which derives its importance,
not from the fact that it is still and small, but because the voice of God—all Deity—lies back of it.
We may, like Elijah, hear the "great and strong
wind," sweeping with the fury of the wild tornado,
and filling land and sea with its violence; but the
Lord may not be in the wind. We may feel the
earthquake, and see mountains move and oceans
lifted, and this not be of so much importance; for
the Lord may not be in the earthquake. We may
see the fire—we may look upon a great volcano in

full eruption, as Vesuvius, when, with a deluge of molten brimstone, it buried Pompeii and Hercula-neum; we may hear the crackling of the flames, and see the hissing lava as it comes plunging, a red river down the steep sides, and hear the bellowing of the mountain's throes, as if ten million furies were rag-ing within,—and yet the Lord not be in the fire. All this may be, not so much God speaking directly, as nature, or God through nature. Now we hear a "still, small voice," the whisper of the Spirit to the soul,—no noise, not even a breath; and then we "veil our faces," for God, the Holy Spirit, is in the "still, *small* voice." That voice, though little, is mightier than tempestuous winds, heaving earth-quakes, and volcanic fires, because a sign, an ex-pression, of something back of it greater than all other things. So, small words and acts are impor-tant, because signs or expressions of great princi-ples.

See that flag. It is a little flag, comparatively. It contains a few yards of cloth, and some red and white and blue stars and stripes on it. Yea, it is dirty, and full of holes and in tatters. And yet, what makes that multitude rend the air with cheers when it appears, and seem beside themselves with excitement? Because it is the star-spangled ban-ner, and belongs to one of the bravest regiments of

the army, and has been through the bloodiest battles of the war. But why should even this make
that little, torn rag so important? Because it is a
sign, a symbol, of mighty principles,—principles
underlying a great government,—principles of liberty, and all that Americans hold dear. And its
bullet-holes and tatters are signs of great battles
fought in defense of those principles. And so in
spiritual concerns. Some little act or word is a sign
of a mighty principle, underlying the infinite government of God.

I look on a little star of brass on the uniform of
an officer, and I think intensely. Why? Because
that little thing is a badge or sign of vast principles
and transactions. I read in that, war. I see through
that, as through an intense magnifying glass, great
armies, tumultuous conflicts, and fields drenched
with gore. As I look through it down the track of
time, from the present to the creation, countless
millions of embattled hosts come tramping before
me, and many garments rolled in blood appear. As
that little star on that uniform is a sign, so that little bauble on that dress is a sign, a sign of a mighty
principle—even pride,—a principle which underlies
all of evil, we may say, in the universe, constituting
the very foundation of hell. I look through that
bauble as through an intense glass, and I see myri-

ads of mighty angels falling from the battlements of heaven down to the bottomless pit. I see a world of worms puffing themselves up against the Almighty, too proud to worship him. I see jealousy, revenge, and many murders. I see millions of dollars used in vain attire and extravagance—ten thousand, to one for religion—while the cause of God goes a-begging, and millions of souls thronging the way to hell perish for the bread of life. I see an awful abyss, crowded with tormented victims; and every spire of flame, as it licks the black vaults of perdition, and curls around the lost, hisses, "Pride, pride has brought these here!"

If little things are so important; if for one little act of impatience and self-will, the great patriarch and law giver was excluded from the goodly land; if for one act of disobedience, Achan, with his family and every living thing he had, was stoned to death; if for one little act, our first parents were thrust from Eden and cursed with disease and death, and the ground cursed for their sake, and the flood-gates of sin and woe opened on this world, and the pit gorged with their fallen posterity; if one violation of God's law, no matter how little, condemns the transgressor as guilty of all; if all this is true— yea, as all this is true—how need we to tremble whose lives have been a series of transgressions, and

those **not** small, but many of them great! How
much, sometimes, is suspended on a little space
of time, and on a little word—a Yes, or No,—
and on a little sentence, or a little act! The dying
thief gasped, "Lord, remember me when thou com-
est into thy kingdom;" and that prayer of nine
words—not taking more than as many seconds to
utter it—changed his destiny forever. In a moment,
he exchanged condemnation for pardon, sin for
holiness, and remorse for peace. In a little while,
he would have been wailing in hell, there to wail
forever; but in a little while, he was rejoicing in
paradise, there to rejoice forever. In a little while,
devils would have snatched his soul and tormented
it eternally; in a little while, angels convoyed it to
the world of glory, there to rise higher than they.
On the threshold of eternity, how little an act of
prayer and faith turned his steps from depths of
woe to heights of bliss! Sinner, such may be your
case if you will.

SERMON VII.

THE WONDERFUL DRESS.

E HEARD a poor widow praising God for a "wonderful dress" he had given her. The daughter of a high ecclesiastic, who was married recently, could not be as much delighted with her dress costing six hundred dollars, with its trail carried by three bearers, as this poor widow was with her wonderful dress. Her raptures set us a-thinking.

God placed man in Eden and put upon him a robe called "original righteousness," which well fitted him in spirit, soul and body, and was most perfect and beautiful.

Man parted with this. One day a lying huckster came along with his infernal wares, and man took off this dress, although he had been faithfully warned and sold it for a little fruit, the eating of which made him deathly sick, and has all his generations.

And now the shame of his nakedness appeared, and he was afraid to meet his Father, and so have been all his children.

The Divine Council knew that man could never enter heaven in such shame, and they, out of infinite mercy, devised another dress for him, called "the robe of Christ's righteousness." God, the Father, planned this; God, the Son, made it; and God, the Holy Ghost, presents and puts it on all who will receive it.

Nothing was ever so opposed as this dress. The being who probably was once next to God and his Son, has made it his sole work for ages to destroy it; he robbed man of his original righteousness in the earthly Eden, and he is determined that he shall never be clothed in the robe of Christ's righteousness and made fit for the heavenly Eden. He is alone stronger than all men together, and he has called to help him legions of fallen angels and the multitude of earth; he has employed the power of great empires to destroy it; he has tried to coax God's children to take it off; to compel them to lay it aside, he has employed ridicule and reproach, and fire and sword; he has kept many from putting it on, and got some to take it off; but thank God many have worn it, and a goodly number now wear it.

Nothing ever cost so much; thousands of years and billions of treasure were spent in its making; a great company of priests and prophets for ages devoted their labor to this alone; the Jewish nation was set apart for this, and all nations contributed; for all their revolutions and counter revolutions were only so many flyings to and fro of the shuttle of providence in weaving it.

It is, so far as we can see, the greatest work that Deity ever has done or can do; all the divine attributes are exhibited in this as in nothing else: omnipotence, in working stupendous miracles, and dashing to pieces great nations who opposed; omniscience, in devising a garment which angels and men and devils must confess, will make the wearer stand complete in the last day; justice, for what can so show God's abhorrence of sin, the filthy rags in which we are clad, and the dreadful vengeance he will wreak upon it, as putting his Son, his equal, in the sinner's place, stripping from him the robes of celestial glory, and casting the filthy rags, foul with our leprosy, upon him; love, God giving his Son, and he saying, "Lo, glad I come."

It was the hardest work that Jesus ever did. He sweat blood; and the blood trickled from his brow crowned with thorns; and those hands wrought so that the blood dropped from them, and those feet too, treading the wine press alone; and that heart was so excited by the mighty labor that it broke. And when it was woven on the mount, then the Spirit of grace held it up before three worlds; and he cried, "It is finished," and hell's dark caverns shook and groaned, "It is finished," and heaven's courts rang with immortal music, "It is finished." And sinner, there he holds it out for you and says, "Come and take it," for it is as free as it is costly and beautiful.

This dress can be worn under all circumstances; at home and abroad, alone and in company, in the closet and in the sanctuary, among the righteous and among the wicked, when the Lord sends us there; in the parlor and in the kitchen, on the farm, in the store, in the shop and in the office, when awake and when asleep, when well and when sick; in a word, under all circumstances. In fine, when once put on it is never to be taken off, never in life, or in death, and through eternity, and no man or devil can get it off without our consent.

This dress thus worn is always convenient, never gets soiled, and is always becoming—that is, in the eyes of God and angels, and saints. We say in the eyes of these, for it has no form nor comeliness in the eyes of the children of this world. They laugh at those who wear it, and deride them as fanatics, crazy fools, separate them from their company, and speak all manner of evil against them falsely. World-lings think more of garments made out of stuff from some plant, or of spinnings from the bowels of a worm, or from some dumb beast's back, than of this robe, planned in the courts of glory, the grandest piece of work ever done by Him by whom were all things made. A dress outcosting and outshining that of kings, and without which no child of Adam can enter the kingdom; but we whom the Lord has cured of worldly folly, sing,

> " Jesus, thy blood and righteousness,
> My beauty are, my spotless dress."

This dress is so perfect that it needs no earthly ornament to set it off. As well might a gewgaw of gold or a diamond be put on the sun. It is durable and strong; like the raiment of the Israelites in the wilderness, it waxeth not old; earth and hell have plucked at it for ages, but cannot start a thread; it shineth as the brightness of the firmament, and as the stars forever and ever.

Let us consider why this dress is needed:

First. In place of our rags. "Take away the fil-thy garments from him." "Behold I have caused thine iniquities to pass from thee, and I will clothe thee with change of raiment." It covers moral nakedness. "I counsel thee to buy of me . . . white raiment that thou mayest be clothed, and that the shame of thy nakedness do not appear."

How will the lost spirit appear in the judgment day, naked in his moral hideousness, exposed to the look of a gazing universe; but oh, what will that be compared to the look of Him whose eyes are as a flame of fire!

This dress conceals deformities—any one looks better when chastely attired. See that beggar child, dirty and in tatters; how disgusting! It is washed and clad; how comely! So with us spiritually. Religion makes the boor and ruffian true gentlemen, for it makes them truly gentle. At the wedding feast this garment makes all alike look shapely and beautiful.

It not only covers but cures. An old story tells of a vestment which cured him who put it on, of whatever disease he had. So this dress has a virtue which heals all the maladies of the soul. It is washed in blood divine, and whatever that touches it cures. All moral leprosy dries up beneath it, and the wounds and bruises and putrifying sores disappear, and the flesh, like that of Naaman, dripping from Jordan, becomes as that of a little child.

It is a family mark—the regalia of the society of Christ. All wear it who come out from among them who are tricked in the fantasies of vanity fair, and become the sons and daughters of the Lord Almighty.

It is our robe of state. The coronation robes of kings and queens, how splendid! stiff with gold and spangled with gems. But here is a robe for a king, a king of that high rank who sing "unto him that loved us, and washed us from our sins in his own blood, and hath made us kings."

It will be the passport in the day of judgment. All, as they come before the bar, will be placed at the right hand or the left, according as they have on this garment or not. Those who would not put on Christ's righteousness will be covered with confusion; there they will stand, a spectacle more hideous than devils who never had the boon offered them. When on earth they mocked those who wore it, and as Paul says, counted them a spectacle and as the filth and offscouring of all things; but the tables are turned, and now they are the spectacle, and counted by God and angels, and even devils, as the filth and offscouring. No matter how highly they carried themselves here; no matter how exalted their church position; no matter how scornfully they treated God's little ones, and greedily swallowed slander against them; no matter how proudly they arrayed themselves in a corrupt world's fashions; in

that day demon's will mock them in their nakedness, and cry, "Why did you not put on the dress so
freely offered, which would have covered all your
shame? Why, even we are ashamed of you; come
now, we have a dress for you, a winding sheet of
fire, come, we will help you put it on; you chose it
on earth, and now you may wear it forever."

But see those on the right hand, clothed in the
fine linen; the great white throne is before them,
and He is upon it, from whose face the earth and
the heaven flee away; worlds are flaming around
them, and yet they are singing—hear them, and
what do they sing?

> " Jesus, thy blood and righteousness
> My beauty are, my glorious dress,
> 'Midst flaming worlds, in these arrayed
> With joy shall I lift up my head."

"After this I beheld, and lo, a great multitude which
no man could number, of all nations and kindreds,
and peoples and tongues, stood before the throne and
before the Lamb, clothed in *white robes*, and palms in
their hands. And one of the elders answered, saying
unto me, what are these which are arrayed in white
robes, and whence came they? And I said unto
him, Sir, thou knowest. And he said unto me,
These are they which came out of great tribulation,
and have washed their robes and made them white

in the blood of the Lamb. Therefore,"—why? Because they are clothed in the white robes. "Therefore, are they before the throne of God and serve him day and night in his temple. And he that sitteth on the throne shall dwell among them. They shall hunger no more, neither thirst any more," because they wear white robes; "neither shall the sun light upon them, nor any heat," for they have clean robes, white robes. "The Lamb which is in the midst of the throne shall feed them, and shall lead them unto fountains of living water, and God shall wipe away all tears from their eyes," for "They have clean robes, white robes, washed in the blood of the Lamb."

This white-robed multitude is in heaven, at the wedding feast, for they have on the wedding garment. They are the church triumphant, the Bride. And "Come hither, I will shew thee the Bride, the Lamb's wife." "And I heard, as it were, the voice of a great multitude, and as the voice of many waters, and as the voice of mighty thunderings, saying, Alleluia, for the Lord God Omnipotent reigneth. Let us be glad and rejoice, and give honor to him; for the marriage of the Lamb is come, and his wife hath made herself ready. And to her was granted that she should be arrayed in fine linen, clean and white, and the fine linen is the righteousness of the saints; and he saith unto me, write, Blessed are they which are called unto the marriage supper of the Lamb;" and only those will be called who have on the wedding garment, THE WONDERFUL DRESS.

SERMON VIII.

THOUGHTS ON PREACHING.

NO ABSOLUTE method of preaching can be devised. Instruction and advice may be very properly given, and these should be heeded with humility and prayer; but after all, the supreme inquiry must be, "Lord, what wilt thou have me to do? I desire to preach the preaching thou dost bid me." Those fully given up to follow God have sometimes grasped the helm with a firm purpose to steer a sermon on a certain course, and the helm has been taken from their hands, while a gulf stream of glory, or a pentecostal wind has swept them quite out of human reckonings, and regions of bliss were discovered, or the beak of truth pierced the hulks of error, and perdition was stirred.

Preaching in the Spirit will not always please or draw. When Jesus preached at Nazareth, "they wondered at the gracious words which proceeded out of his mouth." Then he very unadvisedly add ed a few words (unadvisedly as men see), when his congregation fell into a rage, and led him to the brow of the precipice to cast him down. He uttered some hard sayings, and multitudes turned away to hear him no more.

Stephen preached with the Holy Ghost sent down from heaven. So full was he that his face shone with divine radiance; his congregation gnashed their teeth, ran upon him, and stoned him. It is no infallible sign that a preacher is inspired with the love of Christ, because a multitude run after him, nor that he is not inspired with it because many rage and refuse to hear him. The rule seems to be that the preacher who follows God, will sometimes have a crowd, and sometimes be comparatively forsaken. That man is quite out of order who seeks to say words which will in themselves repel. Only he is in order who trembles under the cross of such preaching, and who feels the girdings of the Holy Ghost when he takes it.

We must study the discourses and teachings of the Master, especially his sermon on the mount, and the Acts and Epistles of the apostles, and the sermons and history of the great reformers and ministers, to find models for preaching.

The mission of the preacher is to bring souls into the kingdom of God, which is "righteousness, and peace and joy in the Holy Ghost;" therefore he should preach the kingdom in all its departments,—the "righteousness," attained by repentance, surrender and faith, and involving pardon, regeneration and entire sanctification; and he must not fail to tell, from a heart running over with Scripture measure, and to demonstrate by a life of holy triumphs, the kingdom "peace and joy"—heaven in the soul here, heaven in the fulness of glory hereafter.

He is the most accomplished preacher who can best sweep the entire key-board of the mighty instrument of redemption, touching those notes which sound forth the harmonies of eternal truth. On the one hand vibrating in sad tone with the wails of the lost and the groans of everlasting despair, and on the other thrilling with the sweeter than seraph song which ascends before the throne. No one man can do this perfectly; therefore the Lord has called men of various qualities and experiences. As Paul says, "And he gave some, apostles; and some, prophets; and some, evangelists; and some, pastors and teachers; for the perfecting of the saints, for the work of the ministry, for the edifying of the body of Christ." This teaches that all preachers are not designed for precisely the same kind of work. True wisdom seeks to help each man in the especial work God has assigned him.

SERMON IX.

THING of great value usually requires great effort and much time to attain it. Holiness, the most valuable of all things to man, is comparatively the most quickly and readily attained.

The Publican said a few words, was justified, and so far made holy; and likewise the penitent thief. An ungodly young man was converted the third day after seeking, and sanctified wholly and filled with the Holy Ghost three days after conversion. We challenge the universe to show a work so mighty accomplished so speedily and easily. Men are sometimes made rich at once by a legacy. The riches of holiness are a legacy, left by Testament, the New Testament, on certain provisos of faith. In the Canaan of perfect love the orchards are already planted and the wells dug, and some sing:

" O that I might at once go up,
No more on this side Jordan stop,
But now the land possess."

Well, stop singing and "go up."

Complete provision has been made for complete salvation from sin now. All the orthodox admit that man must become holy before he enters eternity, if he would enter heaven; then he must become so in this world. And why wait until death since all admit there is no sanctifying power in death, but alone in Christ? And Christ's work is now complete; the vail is rent and all may enter into the holy place. If God can make holy in death, when the mortal struggle is on body and soul, and when "the hour of the power of darkness" often overwhelms, then he can make holy in health, when body and soul are strong. Holiness is needed more in life than in death. What is the chief desire of the saint; to be happy? No, to be holy; to live for God's glory and the spread of his cause; and to do this he must have grace while he lives, not when he dies, for then his work stops. And the more grace he has, even unto holiness or entire sanctification, the more he can do.

We do not fancy this exaltation of death. Death is an enemy, not a saviour; nor in itself any help to salvation. Death is a penalty, a disgrace on a fallen race. Every death is a kind of public execution, before three worlds, by which God testifies his abhorrence of sin. That fragment of existence spent in dying, with holiness written upon it at a snatch, as it were, makes a sorry comparison with a life-time written over with holiness. And such every life-time ought to be, and can be. Oh, this death-bed holiness! it is too much like death-bed repentance.

If it is dangerous to the soul, and a dishonor to grace which has made full provision for holiness now, and an abridgement, if not the nullification, of our ability to work for souls, and a detraction from our enjoyment here, and forever hereafter, to wait until death for holiness—then the same reasons are good against shutting up the experience and enjoyment and practice of holiness to heaven. The power of grace, "the beauty of holiness," is not shown in heaven, where there is nothing from which to save, but by saving now in the place of trial; and the harder the circumstances the more potent and admirable the power that saves.

A man is esteemed according to his competency for present emergencies. Wellington, immediately after winning the battle of Waterloo, was voted a million of dollars and a palace. Why? because he proved himself triumphantly equal to a dire emergency. In this respect holiness demonstrates its power, and exhibits its beauty. It is salvation from sin, all sin, and now, in the battle with earth and hell.

God seems to have elected the hardest place in all his dominions, that is this world, in which to prove the power and the beauty of holiness. He has chosen this to impress upon all intelligences the two most important lessons: first, the ruinous nature of sin; and second, the glory of grace in securing for sinners present holiness right in "this present evil world." And to effect this he has done for this world his greatest work.

God can do for no other world a work so morally grand as he has done for this. He has but one Son, and that Son can die but once. His body being resurrected and glorified, can be touched by death no more. "He liveth evermore;" therefore he can die for no other world. "Herein is love," herein is grace and moral glory beyond compare, that "God gave his Son to die for us."

But I stagger as I think, can we be the subjects of the greatest work of Deity? Is this earth, this speck of creation, groaning and travailing in sin; is this, of all Jehovah's empire, the one spot for this exhibition? Is this space of duration called time, this parenthesis in eternity, the one page in the mighty volume of the universe, written in blood, even the "blood of God;" is this the most wonderful, the most glorious page of all? And this has been done to show the hideousness of sin, and the beauty of holiness. The inhabitants of other worlds read this page. Angels do; for they desire to look into its mystery. Devils do, and believe and tremble. It may be that other intelligences in other stars, like God and angels and devils, are interested in this world more than in any other, because here they behold worked out that most stupendous of problems—sin disposed of in mercy and justice; and here too they see, out of this heap of blackness and ruin, holiness arise, clad in white robes of purity divine. The miracle of the ages is that the redeemed can keep their garments undefiled, not while walking over the gold-paved streets of the New Jerusalem—no virtue in that, for there is no possibility of defilement there—but undefiled and unspotted while walking through the mud and mire and filth of this Sodom. Oh, this is grace, this is holiness, revealing strength and beauty indeed!

Again, complete triumph over Satan and sin is to be manifested in this world. Here Satan has ruined man, and here Christ and holiness are to redeem and reinstate him. Christ is to meet Satan on this earth, which he has usurped, and to destroy his works; first by full and present salvation of the soul from sin and from Satan's rule, and finally by the redemption of the body in the resurrection. Satan has made man, by man's faith in him rather than in God, totally depraved here; Christ can make man, by faith in him rather than in the devil, totally holy or free from sin here. Satan made man sinful instantly. Christ can make him holy instantly. Man was made sinful by yielding to Satan while in life and health, and he lives so for years. Christ can make man holy now, while in life and health, and he can live so for years and constantly. Our Jesus is mightier for good than the devil for evil. Blessed be his name.

SERMON X.

PERSONAL LABOR FOR GOD.

EN are to be saved through the truth; and this can be most effectually presented by the living witness. Very little saving truth is now pressed home upon the conscience. The radical truth, that salvation from sin may be actually and constantly realized in this life, is repudiated by the mass of ministers and professors. Shall we, who have experienced the power of this truth, be idle, while so many are perishing under the cry of "Peace, peace," when there is no peace? God forbid! Forbid it, our own untiring, loving zeal! Let us rather be "instant in season and out of season," to turn aside this tide of infidelity, and pass the full chalice of pure, life-giving truth, to the lips of the perishing millions.

Personal labor promotes the highest spiritual good of the laborer; and, more than this, without it his soul will grow weak and die.

A desire for the salvation of souls, and earnest effort put forth to secure the same, always accompany scriptural conversion—so much so that these are proverbial of the convert. Cessation from these is a mark of backsliding. This desire and effort will cease, of course, unless exercised. So certain as one will sicken and die without physical exercise, so certainly will he die spiritually without spiritual exercise. One cause of so many staggering, ghastly, "crooked-path" professors, is a lack of exercise in the vineyard.

An indolent habit of body and mind, by impairing the general health, begets depression, gloom, and hypochondria. So does spiritual indolence. Some are most of the time under clouds—they almost always have a mournful story to tell. Poor, spiritual hypochondriacs—let them go to work. A brother complained to another, "I am so dry and dead!" The one complained to, said, "Let us make some calls;" and by the time the third call was made, and the third prayer offered, the dry, dead brother's eyes were overflowing with tears and his heart on fire. Such medicine cures.

One of the best preventives and reliefs of coldness is exercise. When boys crowd around the fire, while there is work out-of-doors to do, the father drives them out, and makes them work,—and ere long they are aglow with a warmth much more wholesome and pleasant than that drawn from any stove. So, if any of us feel coldness creeping over our souls, let us not run continually to "the fire," but go to work. And if we hover too much over the old homestead stove, I hope the Father will drive us out into the wide, cold world, and make us work; and then, when we come together, our souls will be radiant and warm.

It is indispensable to be often blessed of the Holy Ghost. No one will long retain spiritual life without this. Yet it is possible to abuse this privilege, and live merely to be blessed—craving the blessing to consume on our lusts for enjoyment; and thus we may become the creatures of a kind of spiritual dissipation—not workers, but *players*, in the vineyard.

The worst forms of fanaticism we ever knew, arose from the notion that the world had become so utterly hardened that no more souls could or would be saved, and therefore God's people were not called to labor any more for this. The persons holding this notion, ceasing from the especial work of the Christian—that is, soul-saving—and still eager to be active in some religious sphere, were set to work by Satan; and, getting their eye off the crosses of Christ, attending the work of soul-saving, Satan imposed on them crosses of his own manufacture, and ran them into notions and practices most absurd and sensual and devilish.

One of the most efficient ways of teaching is by example. It has been remarked that "sinners do not read the Bible much, but they read Christians.' There are very few examples of living Christianity among the multitude of professors. They profess to be separate from the world, but are as intensely after it as any worldling. They follow its fashions of pride and extravagance as fully; and the non-professing worldling truly says, "You are the same as I, except belonging to a church and saying a few prayers." How necessary, then, that those who are really separate from the world, and holy in heart and life, set an example as perfect as possible. "Ye are the light of the world"—not of some one place, but "of *the world.*" Do not cover it up, then, in some bushel of a church or town, but carry it every-where, and thrust it into people's faces, and hold it right around their hearts, that many, "seeing your good works, may be led to glorify your Father in heaven."

We are continually repeating, "The harvest truly is plenteous, but the laborers are few. Lord, send forth laborers." Now, if we really desire this pray-er to be answered, we will try to answer it as the man answered his prayer for the poor—by taking from his store a plentiful supply for them. This alters the case. It is not very difficult to make loud-mouthed petitions that the dark places may be illuminated; but the self-denial involved in going out ourselves, be it in ever so humble a way, is quite a different thing. If men and women after Pentecost, went everywhere preaching the word,—and that amid persecutions we have little idea of, and in places where the art of speaking was carried to a perfection now unequalled—shall we hesitate?

We wonder why the Lord does not, in answer to our pressing importunity, raise up ministers to supply the pressing demand. May not the reason be, that too many of us laity are rusting out, having all that we can do to nurse our own languid piety, which is dying for want of exercise?

And if we should go forth, as our pentecostal brethren and sisters did, God would raise up preachers; and that, too, from among these very Sauls who "breathe out threatenings and slaughters" against us, who would go forth in a "demonstration of the Spirit and of power" that would shake the world.

It is quite natural for church members to gather together, as far as possible, into large societies; concentrating, more for the sake of lightening their burdens than to "contend earnestly for the faith," by battling for its spread over the land. The idea of being "built up in numbers," when made too prominent, carries the idea of an inert mass of church material, which, like so many bricks and sticks and stone, exist only to be "built up." And such, of course, desire only the most accomplished workmen, who will not handle them too roughly, but build them up comfortably and handsomely.

"It is so pleasant to have many brethren and sisters for mutual support and enjoyment; and then we can sustain the means of grace at so much less expense for each one." Shall we ever be possessed with that penurious spirit, which labors to reduce the expense of sustaining the gospel to the least possible minimum, lest the purse have a little strain? And the more the number of members increases, the greater the avidity to have the reduction go on, until the real ruling motive is, not an increase of members, that souls may be saved, but that expense may be saved. God forbid that we should ever be possessed with such a spirit! There is, however, strong temptation to it, where a large number of members crowd together. It does not require a large church to abundantly support the means of grace, when that church is filled with the Spirit of Him "who, although rich, yet for our sakes became poor."

There is danger of leaning on a large church.

"Oh, we shall surely succeed," says one, "because we have such a large and excellent church." And so says another, and so each one throughout—leaving all for "the church" to do; forgetting that a church is made up of units, and if each one counts naught, the whole sum is naught.

A bad feeling is apt to be generated in large societies, concentrated more for the sake of mutual support and enjoyment, than for self-denial and cross-bearing. Heat and feverishness result from this over-crowded state; then fermentation; and all the tact of the most skillful ecclesiastical doctor, is taxed to prevent an explosion or decomposition from the gases of discord, while scarcely a soul is saved from without. The usual result, however, is that the whole concern dries up, and becomes a mummy of formalism, all duly laid out and embalmed. This concentrating and crowding is very liable to produce suffocation; the Wind of Heaven has not free scope. "What makes it so close in this old, big church?" says one from the cabins on the frontier; "it seems as though I would choke. There are too many of you crowded in here. Go out and ventilate yourselves on the broad prairies, and in the woods and waste places."

A family of genuine piety are about to change their residence. Their chief motive, of course, is their own spiritual good and that of others. Now, how can this be best secured? By going to a place where there is a large and strong church, or to one where there is a very weak church, or none at all? Why should they go where the strong church is? To be helped? or to help? It is supposed that strong churches do not need helping continually; and one of the best ways to become strong. if weak, is to help others. It may be said, "We have friends and kindred where the strong church is." That weighs but little with him, who would not allow one who proposed to follow him to go home to bury his own father. "Our temporal interests will be best promoted there." This may very properly be a consideration, but one utterly subordinate to the one of, "Where can I do the most good?" Still, you are good for five or ten years in the vineyard yet. You need, perhaps, more of the spirit of the old man who, at eighty, visited and prayed with every family in a town of five thousand, and established and led a weekly prayer meeting, and saw as the result hundreds saved. At eighty-two he went to live in a town of twenty-five hundred; and there he visited and prayed with every family, and then took an everlasting visit to the glory-world.

Go to some place where the gospel, in its purity, is not preached, and where there are but few real

Christians. The land is full of such places, and
from more than one the cry goes up, "Come over
and help us." Go there; start a prayer-meeting in
your own house if need be,—and invite your neighbors to come in. Go to their homes and invite
them, and you will soon have a house full. Talk to
them there from a heart burning with divine love—
and I think that, under such circumstances, it will
burn. Ere long, souls will be saved. And how you
yourself will be revived! How fresh and strong you
will become! a very giant, refreshed with new wine;
for then the Master will hand it out, and fill your
cup to overflowing. Before many months you will
send for a minister; and you will, if need be, and
you are able, gladly support him alone. Such work
will make you feel wonderfully rich. A salvation
church will be formed, and the work permanently
rooted. But be careful not to settle down at this
point. Break up, if you can, and go to do a similar
work in another place; and keep itinerating until
really superannuated. The itinerating would not be
confined to ministers, if many lay-men and women
did their duty. We need more of the spirit of him,
familiarly known in our borders as "Uncle Zack,"
who did a good work in York state, then came to
Illinois in his old age, and helped to do a glorious
work there; and the last we knew of the old man,

he said he "wanted to pull up stakes and go to Iowa," where, to use one of his own eccentric sayings, "he will jump right onto the altar, and scratch off live coals until the prairies are all a-fire." The old patriarch seems bound to carry out the spirit he had when first converted, "When", he says, "I felt as though I wanted to run till I'd carried the news to the other end of creation, and then jump off into glory." And soon he will. And I pray God, that each one of us will run to carry the good news, and run, and run, until we get under such headway, that at last we shall clear the river of death at a bound, and leap into the very heart of glory.

What incentives to personal labor for God! those already mentioned; and then the commands, as, "Whatsoever thy hand findeth to do, do it with thy might"; and the promises, as, "He that goeth forth and weepeth, bearing precious seed, shall doubtless come again with rejoicing, bringing his sheaves with him." Think of Jesus: he labored personally; he did not save us by proxy—by an angel, or all angels—"who gave *himself* for us." We are to be judged according to our *"deeds."*—"Who will render to every man according to his deeds, to those who by patient continuance in *well-doing*, seek for glory and honor and immortality, eternal life." If the Master has bestowed ten talents, five, or one, they must be used. Shall we hear, "Thou wicked and slothful servant"? wicked, because slothful. Shall the Judge say this to us, and souls lost through our sloth wail it forever in our ears? Shall no soul be saved through us? Shall we meet no immortal spirit in the paradise of God to welcome us, and while he clasps our hand, say, "Through you, under Jesus, I am here, saved from yonder burning pit, and ranging the fields of the blest"? Shall we barely get to heaven ourselves? Shall we have a crown, but no stars in it?

> " If grief in heaven might find a place,
>   And shame the worshiper bow down,
> Who meets the Saviour face to face;
>   'Twould be to wear a starless crown.
>
> To find in all that countless host
>   Who meet before the eternal throne—
> Who once, like us, were sinners lost—
>   Not one to say, 'You led me home.'
>
> Oh! may it ne'er of me be said,
>   No soul that's saved by grace divine
> Has called for blessings on my head,
>   Or linked its destiny with mine."

Forbid it, Almighty God! Forbid it, our own holy diligence! But, when we enter those celestial courts, may many rise up to call us "blessed," and many stars beam from our crown of rejoicing.

SERMON XI.

PORTION OF A SERMON ON NOAH'S ARK.

OR one hundred and twenty years Noah preached to the antediluvians and told them of their awful wickedness and the coming flood. Some laughed, some mocked, some raged, some said, "It may come, but there is plenty of time to get ready." Finally, being warned of God, Noah commenced preparing an ark. He laid the first timbers. The country around wondered what he was about. He was giving them practical proof that he believed what he preached. The work went on. The gopher trees fell in the woods, as scores of axes rang out in the hands of the sturdy workmen. The voices of the teamsters were heard as they urged on their teams. The thud of hammer and axe sounded as piece after piece was shaped and put together. And so the strange structure

294

went up. The news spread, and multitudes came to see. The common talk ran like this, most probably:

"An old fellow, who has been harping on our wonderful wickedness and warning us against a wonderful flood for the last hundred years, has put the cap on his folly by beginning to build a boat to save himself and family in. He cannot be a fool, for he shows great skill in building this boat, and uncommon power in warning the people, so much so that a large number are about out of their wits on account of his preaching. He can scarcely be called crazy, for there is too much method in his madness. The ship-builders who have examined his ark pronounce it a master-piece for the purpose designed. He must be set down, then, as a fanatic. This appears from the following considerations: first, he has been telling this story for the last hundred years, and there are no more signs of a flood than when he began; second, he is building the thing on high land, fifty miles from any water large enough to float it; third, he is using up all his means on this huge folly, and will most likely soon be on the town. We seriously believe our king would do a good service to him and his family, and to the world of mankind at large, by shutting him up for a season, or for life if need be, for most likely he will never recover from this hallucination, as it has been on him over a hundred years and is manifestly growing worse."

But Noah went on, for God permitted no one to hinder him. The ark was finished—five hundred and twenty-five feet from stem to stern, eighty-seven and one-half feet beam. and fifty and one-half feet from keel to hurricane deck,—an astonishment then and also now.

Now came the most wonderful part. Noah and his wife, and Shem, Ham and Japheth with their wives go into the ark; and then all kinds of animals by twos and by sevens come trooping in after, "and they went in unto Noah into the ark." One would think that this would have convinced those cavillers Noah was right. No, no more than the astonishing miracles of Jesus did the apostate Jews that he was right. They trumped up some way to account for it. Perhaps they remarked, "Why, don't you know that our jugglers charm snakes and draw them from their holes? So this Noah has struck some law by which he draws these beasts and birds." Perhaps he mesmerized them, the same as the Free Methodists are said to do nowadays in drawing persons into their strange way.

All the animals are in—the elephants in their stall and the camelopards in theirs, the lions in their cage, the mouse in his nest, and the eagle and chipping bird on their roost,—all are in. Then God takes hold of the great door with his great hand and brings it tight shut; "and the Lord shut him in."

A multitude perhaps were around to witness the entrance of Noah and his family and the beasts into the ark; for they all entered in one day. The word says, "In the selfsame day entered Noah and his family, they and every beast after his kind; and the Lord shut him in." For a moment the crowd may have been startled at the echo of the great door as it flew shut, and as they gazed on the huge structure, without a sign of life on the outside yet so full of life within. They gazed a moment in stillness; then, prompted by a spirit of satanic defiance against Noah and his warnings and ark, they sent up an infernal yell mingled with laughter and taunts, and a shower of stones rained on the ark's side. But the only effect of that was to scare the deer and the camelopards a little.

They doubtless had the same spirit as other crowds who pressed on Wesley and others of God's servants; and they cried, "Halloo, old fellow! come out and show yourself. What are you doing in that big tub with your menagerie? Come, open the door; we want to go into the show. Can't you preach us another sermon about the flood? it seems more like

a drought just now. Ha, ha! give us a little something to drink. We're cursed dry; give us a little
wet—give us a flood. Yes, a flood; anything's better than this dry."

Noah said not a word; but he doubtless prayed
during this time.

Now goes up a cry more alarming than any before,—"Fire, fire! bring fire! Ha, ha, what a bon-
fire this will make, all covered with pitch inside and
out!"

Noah's wife now becomes seriously alarmed.
"Why, father," she says, "they will burn us up."
And Shem, Ham and Japheth and their wives grow
pale and tremble. They say, "Father, don't you
think that after all you are mistaken?"

"No," calmly replies the old man; "God don't
lie."

Finally, when the vast crowd had become one
mob determined to destroy the ark, when perhaps
with yells they were rushing with torches to fire it,
then—all at once, not gradually—the flood came;
for it says, "In the six hundredth year of Noah's
life, in the second month, the seventeenth day of
the month, *the same day* were all the fountains of
the great deep broken up, and the windows of heav-
en were opened." As in the day of the coming of
the Son of man, he shall come as suddenly as the

lightning shineth from the east to the west, so suddenly burst the flood upon a world ripe for ruin. The firmament rent by ten thousand lightnings cracked and fell. The earth heaved, and the mighty ocean was flung against the highest mountains, and curled in foam around their loftiest peaks. Subterranean seas burst the earth's crust, and whole cities sank like a stone. The mocking mass encompassing the ark beat against its sides, and cried and yelled for admittance. But the door was shut.

And so it will be against you, sinner, in that day when a flood of fire shall swim around this globe. In those days there were all kinds destroyed. Some were open scoffers, some raged against the truth, some were subtile reasoners and prided themselves on their cool philosophy, and some were good-natured neglecters; but all were alike engulfed.

How they worked to save themselves!—if they had worked half as earnestly before, all would have been saved. They looked to the ark, safely floating; but the door was shut. Then they fled to the highest hills. Some climbed the mountains until they got among the eternal snows and glaciers, but all in vain. Twenty-seven feet above the tallest mountain top the waters prevailed. They looked from their dizzy heights upon the rising flood, chasing them as a relentless tiger chases his prey; and then again they looked at the distant ark floating in perfect safety, and longed to be there; but the door was shut.

So will you, sinner, in that day when God shall rain on his enemies an horrible tempest, and fire and brimstone, look on the Ark of Salvation, filled with happy saints; *but the door will be shut.* When you stand at the judgment bar, and hear that sentence, "Depart from me, ye cursed, into everlasting fire, prepared for the devil and his angels," the bellowing thunders of hell, yawning to receive you, will sound upon your ears, and devils hissing and shrieking will rush upon you to take you as their prey. You will run this way and that; but the door will be shut, *forever shut.* Only one door will be open then—the door of the bottomless pit; and in you will go. And when the last one is cast in, and that old dragon the devil, their master, then the door of hell will be shut; no devil or sinner will ever go forth to trouble God's universe more.

The ark was large enough to contain a vast number—all animals of all kinds, by twos and by sevens. So the Ark of Salvation is large enough to contain a vast number—all the world in fact. Three hundred million passengers, from the time of Adam down to this, have got aboard; and yet there is room. Millions will get aboard during the millen-

nium—that one thousand or three hundred thousand
years when the human race will so increase, and almost all get aboard.

Think of that scene. The history of the world is
ended. Millions, yea billions, are aboard; not
crowded aboard, for there is plenty of room—nothing stinted about this Ark. The final flood comes.
The fountains of the great deep break up, crashing
thunders rend from pole to pole. The winds of
vengeance are let loose, and billows of fire roll. See
the old Ship ride! for she is fire-proof as well as
water-proof. She outrides the storm, while the
flimsy, bass-wood crafts of infidelity burn and go
under.

She sees the last one sink, and then her Pilot
turns her prow for the continent of glory. See her
go! Her timbers are Jachin and Boaz, strength established; her deck is inlaid with pearl and gold;
her masts like polished ivory; her sails of fine linen,
like the wings of angels. Right on she speeds. All
on board are sweetly singing, "Glory, hallelujah!"
Won't shouts go up then? No velvet-eared formalists there, who can swallow a whole camel of worldly noise and nonsense at a gulp, but choke to death
over one little "Glory to God!"

Hallelujah! the mountains of Zion are looming
up, the towers of the city appear, the golden shore

is visible, and a thousand forms are hovering there.
Right on she speeds; up the river of life we go, the
orchards of paradise on either side.   The very
branches sweep the deck, and the apples of life roll
all around.   Down come the sails.   The port is
made. Safe, safe at home! The bells of the city
ring; and the King, with ten thousand times ten
thousand angels, comes down and gives us welcome.
Out pour the passengers. See the millions, hear
them singing!

Friends will you be there? You may. There is
room in the glorious old Ark for you; yes, a state-
room, all furnished. Come, come to the door! Remember there is only one door. It is strait, yet
wide enough for all creation to go through,—three
thousand went through in one day once. Come!
you shall have a ticket free for the asking, and fare
that angels would like to feast on.

SERMON XII.

WITNESSES AT THE JUDGMENT.

THE hour has come; all is ready. The Judge is on the bench; the parties are in court— and it opens.

No lawyers will be there,—we mean, no one to manage cases. There will be no need of them; they might only darken counsel, as they often do here. As in some high courts of equity, the judges simply examine testimony and decide from that, so in this the highest court of equity.

The judgment rendered will be fair. The Judge knows all things, and cannot be deceived or err. He is honest. He cannot be tempted by bribery or greed of gain, for he owns all things. He cannot be frightened or moved by fear; he is the Almighty. He knows no partiality; "the Judge of all the earth will do right." He is love; he will give no sentence but that which the highest good of all souls demands. He is angry against nothing but sin.

The Revelator in his vision of the Judgment says, "And the books were opened, and the dead were judged out of those things which were written in the books."

One book will be *the gospel.* Jesus says, "He that rejecteth me and receiveth not my words, hath one that judgeth him: the word that I have spoken, the same shall judge him in the last day."—John 12:48. This word, or gospel, includes the law, that is, the threatenings and precepts as well as promises of grace; for God says by Paul, "As many as have sinned in the law shall be judged by the law;....in the day when God shall judge the secrets of men by Jesus Christ according to my gospel."—Rom. 2:12, 16. Do we obey this gospel, as taught in the "Sermon on the Mount" for instance; or, do we say, "Lord, Lord," and do not the things which he commands us? Do we deny ourselves, even cutting off offending hands and feet, as the gospel requires? Do we "love not the world, neither the things which are in the world"? Are we separate from the world? No matter who you are, or how you feel, if you obey not this gospel, you will be condemned by it in that day "when the Lord Jesus shall be revealed from heaven with his mighty angels, in flaming fire taking vengeance on them that know not God, and that obey not the gospel of our Lord Jesus Christ." —2 Thess. 1: 7, 8.

The blessings of providence will witness against the sinner. One book is *divine providence*. Paul says, "Or despisest thou the riches of his goodness and forbearance and longsuffering; not knowing that the goodness of God leadeth thee to repentance? but after thy hardness and impenitent heart treasurest up unto thyself wrath against the day of wrath and revelation of the righteous judgment of God?"—Rom. 2: 4, 5. Every mouthful of food; every day and night; the sun with its light and heat; the beauties of nature; the privileges of society, of education and books, and means of intelligence; the improvements of art and science; the enjoyments of family and home,—all will rise up to condemn and curse the sinner in that day. His greatest blessings now will be his greatest curses then.

Another book of testimony will be *conscience*. No man can put in the plea, "I have not had the Scripture to teach me"; for God says, "For when the Gentiles, which have not the law, do by nature the things contained in the law, these having not the law, are a law unto themselves: which show the work of the law written in their hearts, their conscience also bearing witness, and their thoughts the meanwhile accusing or else excusing one another."—Rom. 2:14, 15. Men have declared that when in the jaws of death, all the sins of their lives flashed before them; so in the Judgment a quickened conscience will bring out of the past the memory of every sin.

Angels may witness,—"Yes, Lord, thou didst appoint me a guardian for this soul, and I followed him for years, trying to lead in paths of purity, but he chose to hear to his own heart, and to devils, until he died without God and without hope." And *devils* may witness,—"Yes, Lord, that is so."

The lost may witness against one another and say, "Yes, O God; I heard that man blaspheme. I was by when he did that lustful and hellish deed. I knew of that dishonest act. I tempted him and he tempted me, and hand in hand we went on defying thee."

Saints may witness. The mother may witness against the son,—"Yes, Lord; I prayed for him, I pleaded with him: thou knowest and he knows my tears and groans." Husbands may witness against wives and wives against husbands. That wife whose husband was a local preacher, making high professions, sometimes crying or shouting, and yet acting the devil in his family, raging and speaking vulgar words; who stood between his wife and the narrow way, ridiculing her neat but plain dress, refusing to be seen walking the streets with her on account of it,—himself decked with gold and jewelry,—harrassing her until she gave up in despair and said, "It is no use; he is dragging me to hell"—that wife and those children will witness against that man.

The faithful minister may witness,—"Lord, thou knowest I did not shun to declare unto these thy whole counsel." And lost souls may witness against the unfaithful minister,—"O God, that man was my preacher. He knew, if he knew anything as he should, that I disobeyed thy word, that I was the creature of worldliness, or pride, or covetousness; and he through blindness, or fear of losing salary or place, let me go quietly down to hell."

The *Holy Spirit* will witness. Then the lost may think of the hymn commencing,

> " Stay, thou insulted Spirit, stay."

But they will repeat it then,

> " Yea, thou insulted Spirit, yea—
>   Oh, I have done thee such despite,
> Now thou dost cast me quite away
>   To dwell in everlasting night."

> " For I did steel my stubborn heart,
>   And banish all my guilty fears,
> And vex and urge thee to depart,
>   Through many long rebellious years."

The Spirit will say, "Yes, that is true."

The *Judge himself* will be an infallible witness. A

criminal told an attorney all about his capital crime. Sometime after he came into court for trial, and as soon as he saw the judge grew ghastly pale; for he was that attorney lately elected judge. When asked, "Guilty, or not guilty?" he tremblingly answered, "Guilty"; for he knew the judge knew all about his sin. So will it be with sinners at the Judgment in that day.

SERMON XIII.

A PECULIAR PEOPLE.

FOR thou art an holy people unto the Lord thy God, and the Lord hath chosen thee to be a peculiar people unto himself, above all the nations that are upon the earth.—Deut. 14:2.

God's people are peculiar because they have a peculiar religion.

Various religions prevail. One has no God, as Atheism; others profess to have a God, but no Christ; as Mahommedanism, Paganism, Spiritualism. Another professes high reverence for God and Christ, but conveys no salvation from actual sin, as Popery. This warrants salvation from the guilt of sin, through confession to a priest, and through absolution and penance, and buying the soul out of purgatory; while allowing the man to live as wicked as the devil wants him to. This kind may be styled that of salvation in sin. Under this head must be ranged all nominally orthodox people who maintain that they have salvation. From what—sin or sinning? Many profess to be saved from sin, meaning by that guilt, who scout the idea of being saved from sinning, as though salvation from sin did not necessarily include salvation from sinning as the fountain includes its streams. These retort, "Oh, I don't pretend to be perfect, or to live without sin." Then, they have salvation in sin, like the Papist. "Oh," say they, "I believe in Christ as my Savior." And so, too, says many an ungodly Universalist. They have no saving faith in Jesus; for he saves his people from their sins.

The votaries of another kind of religion profess to be saved from sin while manifestly they are not saved from the world, from its spirit, love, fashions and customs. "I am saved from sin," say they, in a pretty way. "I enjoy perfect love." No; for you are not saved from the world. "Oh, yes, I am." Take down your sign then. "Oh! but we must be attractive to the world." These trimmers act the same in principle as the Papists, who would convert the heathen by incorporating Pagan rites with their own,—as baptizing converts in the Ganges, because they esteem it a sacred stream; and encouraging them to carry the image of the Virgin through the streets, as they do Juggernaut. So, this kind takes

converts into the church with all their idols. They
lower the standard to suit their own lusts, and then
measuring themselves by it, profess to live without
sin. These "turn the truth of God into a lie," and
"the grace of God into lasciviousness."

God's people are peculiar, because their religion is
different from these kinds which rule in the earth.
It has a Jesus in it in all the power of his name. It
saves them from that abominable species of sin
denounced by God as "adultery," namely, friendship
for the world. Jas. 4:4. Their Savior gave himself
for their sins, that he might save them from this
present evil world.

God's people are peculiar in religious manifestations.
Those of the world are in earnest. What wonder
then that his are, when interests the most tremendous engage them. Have the people of the world
fears—fears of disaster, disease, death? What are
these compared to fears of hell, of everlasting woe?
Are they in earnest lest opportunity for gain of
money or honor slip? No marvel then that God's
people are, lest opportunity for the salvation of a
soul slip; for another opportunity may be found to
retrieve temporal loss; but that soul may never find
another for eternal gain. Are worldlings excited
over truths delivered by the political speaker or popular lecturer, and cheer, and clap hands, and stamp,

laugh or weep? And shall it be counted strange
that saints shout and even leap, when he who spake
as never man spake, pours through head and heart,
in the power of the Holy Ghost, a flood of truth
pertaining to interests beside which the most thrilling perishable concerns are a vapor. Must they
thunder with voice and cannon over some victory
of blood and butchery, and then find fault that
saints are demonstrative, when by "the fight of
faith" a victory is achieved through which an
immortal is turned from sin to purity, from Satan
to Jesus, from hell to heaven?

*God's people are peculiar in not living in the same
world with those of this.* What is the world? not soil
and landscape merely, but, essentially, thoughts,
affections and actions. Our Lord says of his people, "Ye are not of the world." Paul says of them,
"Our conversation," that means citizenship, "is in
heaven." He also says, "But ye *are* come unto
Mount Zion, and unto the city of the living God,
the heavenly Jerusalem, and to an innumerable company of angels." That is, ye are now, spiritually
speaking, in the world where the mount lifts its
majestic head, and the city stands, and the angels
live. In a mystical, and yet delightful sense, the
prediction has been accomplished for us, or rather
in us, of "a new heaven and a new earth;" for a

kingdom is set up within us. The prophecy of
Esaias has come to pass in our world: "For brass I
will bring gold, and for iron I will bring silver. Our
walls are salvation and our gates praise. The sun
shall be no more thy light by day, [that is sunlight
is insignificant by the side of this God-light]; neither
for brightness shall the moon give light unto thee,
[that is the light and glory poured upon us in the
night, at our evening meetings, totally eclipses the
brightest moon]; but the Lord shall be unto thee an
everlasting light, and thy God thy glory. Thy sun
shall no more go down."

The peculiar people inhabit a world of occupa-
tions, fashions and language different from those of
this. What is your business, citizen of the saint-
world? I "follow," as a business, "peace with all
men, and holiness, without which no man shall see
the Lord." Our standard of fashion is not the wild,
unchaste, unwholesome fancies of a set of French
and Dutch popinjays, but that blessed word which
says, "Whether ye eat or drink, or whatsoever ye do,
do all to the glory of God." The people of the sin-
world do not understand the language of the peculiar people, any more than a Hottentot who has
never seen a book understands the word book. The
peculiar people shout the word "glory." Worldlings
laugh at it; they do the same as an American smiles

at the jargon of a Chinaman; because it is an unmeaning term to them, it is a foreign language, that of another world; it is the expression and sign of a glory in the soul, of which they have no conception.

The people of God are peculiar in working on a different base-line from those of the world. The importance of a base-line in military movements is well known. The same is true in business. One man succeeds remarkably, while another, equally sagacious and energetic, fails; the difference is to be found in the business base-line. This nation started with a base-line warped by slavery. An awful war was the consequence. Spiritual interests are the most vital; worldlings do not see this. God's people do, because they look from another standpoint. The base-line of the worldling runs along "the plain," low down, among the fogs; they cannot see afar off; that of saints, over Mount Zion. They "stay not in all the plain," but have escaped to the Mountain, where the air is clear and the prospect wide. They see sinners standing on the crumbling edge of the flaming gulf. They see mighty powers pushing them off —disease, pestilence, war, death in its myriad shapes, —all the evil forces of earth and hell. There! there! they are falling, thousands, every day, and thousands are tottering on the brink; but God is holding them a little longer, for Mercy pleads. The base-line of the worldling is self. God is not in all his thoughts, to love and fear. That of the peculiar people is God. They tread softly along this line. They would welcome death sooner than offend. Worldlings everywhere, out of churches and in, trim from public opinion, saints from divine. The base-line of the one is run in reference to eternity. Eternity! Eternity, thrills through their spirits; the other for time and sense. The one seek a city here, and never find it; the other, a city out of sight, and shall find it; for it hath foundations which nothing of this world has.

God's people are peculiar in their estimate of value. They count this world, out of Christ, with all its grandeur, of little value, of no final value—yea, ultimately worse than worthless. They believe that without repentance none can escape hell. Very few do repent. Of what worth then for eternity will multitudes be? They have sold themselves for naught. The day is coming when the earth shall be burned, and all the magnificent works of men consumed. Will they not be valueless then? Yes, a curse; for they are idols, which will only sink their worshipers lower into the pit. Babylon was great. Of what value is it now? And of what account is all the ancient mightiness of her kings and people, while they are wailing in perdition? Of what worth is a world whose prince—yea, whose god, is such a monster as the devil? He is called "the prince" and "the god of this world", because rebels against the King of kings and Lord of lords, elect him. Of what value is a world of slaves to the meanest of masters—the most abject of slaves—"taken captive by the devil at his will"? No wonder that the Great Arithmetician, whose eye takes in creation at a glance, and who knows the value of each figure in its mighty columns, and can add them without mistake,—no wonder that he said, "What is a man profited if he gain the whole world and lose his own soul? or what shall a man give in exchange for his soul?" He could calculate the worth of that soul, too. He saw the lines of its value running out through eternity, high as heaven, deep as hell.

See those scales suspended over the universe. All the world, all its riches and glory are cast into one balance. The Son of God stands by; a soul has just left the body, he stops it on its passage, and places it in the empty balance, and as the other rises like a feather, he cries with a voice which thrills heaven and startles hell, "What shall a man give in exchange for his soul?" And angels sing, "What shall a man give in exchange for his soul?" And the redeemed in glory, as they look to the pit from whence they were digged, and then look around those plains of delight,—shout with hallelujahs above angels, "What shall a man give in exchange for his soul?" And the lost soul, as it is dragged to the pit, more horrible than that of mire and clay, lined with quenchless fires, as it sees the bursting flames, shrieks, "What is a man profited if he gain the whole world and lose his own soul?" and as it sinks down, down, forever down, we hear ascending from the cavern of the damned, "What is a man profited if he gain the whole world and lose his own soul?" And the mighty ones of earth with all the nations that forget God rise up to meet him, and join in the chorus of eternal despair, "What is a man profited if he gain the whole world and lose his own soul?"

HOME.

A PILGRIM passes through this earth. Devils like Russian wolves are howling on his track. The world casts smut upon him. He comes to the river of death, plunges in and rises with a shout on the other side.

His guardian angels, who have convoyed him all the way from infancy, now conduct him to heaven, and cry as they approach, "Lift up your heads, O ye gates; and be ye lifted up, ye everlasting doors."

The gates spring open. He walks up the gold-paved streets. He sees an angel standing there with his face like the sun, his wings like snow, a trumpet by his side and a harp in his hands. One of his guardian angels leads him forward and says, "Gabriel, I have the honor of introducing to you one of the Lord's saints."

Gabriel says, "All hail, thou blessed of the Lord."

Pilgrim replies, "How do you do, Gabriel; I am

glad to see you. I've heard of you very often on earth."

"Yes," says Gabriel, "no doubt; and I have noticed you many a time among the pilgrims there. Where are you going to now?"

"Thou knowest, Gabriel."

"Well, you are going up higher, into the throne."

"How do you feel about that Gabriel, my going higher than you; are you not a bit jealous?"

Gabriel takes his harp and begins to sing, "Worthy is the Lamb——." And as he sings pilgrim begins to climb. He leaves the angels and climbs, climbs, where angel foot never trod nor wing waved, —up, above, "*far* above all principality," where God lives, sits enthroned. And as the angels see him they join in with Gabriel and sing, "Worthy is the Lamb that was slain to receive power, and riches, and wisdom, and strength, and honor, and glory, and blessing."

Pilgrim turns around, and looking down upon them joins with them. Then he takes up a strain at which they all stop, and he sings alone, "Unto him that loved us, and washed us from our sins in his own blood, and hath made us kings and priests unto God and his Father; to him be glory and dominion forever and ever." And every glorified saint on the mount of God catches up the strain, "To him be

glory and dominion forever and ever. Amen."
And as it rolls among the hills and vales of heaven,
the angels stand still leaning on their harps and
whisper, "Heaven never heard such music before."

I intend to emigrate to that country; it is so
healthy and wealthy, the society is so pure and
friendly, and the light there is so unsullied. We
hear about the cloudless sky of Italy, the lucid
atmosphere and the gorgeous sunsets. But I know
of a clime which has a purer atmosphere. No
thunder-clouds ever roll across that sky, nor lightnings flash. There are no gorgeous sunsets; for
there the Sun never goes down.

I love music. I love to hear an accomplished
band. I love to hear God's children sing in the
Spirit, making melody in their hearts unto the
Lord. Such music to me has seemed almost overwhelming sometimes at camp meetings. To be off
alone in the grove, and all at once to hear hundreds
of saints unite in some song of Zion, surpasses any
music I ever heard. But to be wandering among
the groves of that land, and while seated under
some tree of life to hear the company of those who
have come out of great tribulation and washed their
robes and made them white in the blood of the
Lamb, with glorified bodies, with glorified lungs
which never tire, and glorified voices without a flaw,

clear as a trumpet of silver; to hear this multitude
singing, while the angels drop their harps to listen,
and the arches of the glory world tremble as the
waves of melody like the voice of many waters roll
around them,—that, that is music! such as "ear
hath not heard," "neither hath entered into the heart
of man," such as "God hath prepared for them that
love him."

I want to go to that land. I am going, and as I
travel I sing,—

> "I'm but a stranger here;
> Heaven is my home."

There we shall see those who have gone before.
We shall see the father and mother of us all. We
shall shake the hand of Enoch, that hand which
never grew cold in death. We shall talk with Noah
about his boat ride, and how he felt while sailing
over the tops of the mountains. We shall sit down
in that Kingdom with the glorious patriarchs, Abraham, Isaac and Jacob. We shall look up into the
face of the meek, giant-minded Moses, that face
which was so bathed in Deity that Israel could not
look upon its dazzling radiance. We shall take a
ride with Elijah in his chariot of fire. We shall see
the three fire-proof brethren and hear Daniel the
prophet speak. We shall see the blessed apostles,

the brethren and sisters of the ancient church and the millions of martyrs. We shall look on the rugged, mountain face of Luther, his eyes sparkling like diamonds in two deep mines. We shall see Wesley the king of itinerants who, very likely, following out his old bent, will be planning an excursion to the four quarters of the universe. We shall see them all, and also those dear by kindred ties. We shall hail those whose bodies we laid away in the cold grave,—that babe, that child, that son and daughter who left us in the flush of youth, that mother, that father, that companion and friend. They died in Jesus. Angels conveyed them to that land. There, in bodies all glorious—there, in robes celestial—there, with hearts which shall never throb with sorrow, with eyes which shall never shed a tear—there in LIFE ETERNAL,—there, we shall hail them, no more to die, no more to part.

Ever Yours,
M. F. La Due

MEMOIR

OF

MRS. M. F. LA DUE.

MRS. MARTHA FRANCIS LA DUE.

LTHOUGH feeble in health when the preparation of Mr. La Due's life was commenced, it is not probable that at that time his wife supposed her own memoir would follow his, and in the same volume. But in the providence of God she has been called up higher, and we feel it but fitting to give to her many friends, and others who may read these pages, some account of her life.

Mrs. Martha Francis La Due was born August 24, 1826, in Manheim, Oneida County, New York.

She was a daughter of Rev. John H. and Mary S. Wallace, and the oldest of five children, all of whom she outlived by many years.

When about two years old she narrowly escaped drowning. Near her father's house was a large, deep spring. She was forbidden to draw water from it alone; but her desire to be like the older members of the household led her into disobedience one day, and as a result she fell into the spring, from which she was taken in an unconscious condition. But her life was mercifully preserved, God having in store for her many years of labor in his vineyard.

Her early training was of the strictest Methodist kind, yet not unaccompanied with much tenderness. No visiting was allowed on Sunday, no one could board or stay in the family who would not kneel at family prayers, no ornaments were allowed to be bought or accepted as gifts, and all were required to attend church and otherwise properly observe the Sabbath. Thorough obedience was insisted on by her father, and punishment though not often inflicted, was sometimes severe. She did not complain of the manner in which she was brought up, but approved it as one of the chief means by which she was prepared to submit her heart to God and to bear the yoke of Christ.

She had a good education, considering her circumstances as the daughter of a Methodist itinerant preacher. She studied at home, and in select school, also in a school taught by her father, and in Lima Seminary. She read and parsed in Pollock's Course of Time, and studied rhetoric, before she was twelve. Wesley's Journals and D'Aubigne's History of the Reformation were among her favorite early books;

and while yet quite a young woman she was passionately fond of Butler's Analogy, parts of which work she believed to have specially influenced her entire life.

A considerable part of her religious experience we are able to give in her own words, as follows:

"At the age of fourteen, I was awakened and converted to God. From a child of five years, I had been the subject of deep convictions for sin; and when my mother took me alone to pray with me, as was her custom almost daily, I often felt an inexpressible sense of the presence of a holy God, and the infinite compassion of Jesus. My heart sometimes felt strangely warm, even burning at the mention of the name of Jesus. But these feelings were transient and easily overcome. They were simply good desires.

"During the winter of my conversion, there was a general revival in the church I attended, and all over the circuit of C———, then embracing many societies. Several of my associates were clearly converted before I began to feel the burden of my sins; but the night I started to seek God, all about me were indifferent, and I saw if I was to save my soul I must be willing to go *alone*. The invitation being given, I arose from near the back part of the church in the midst of many unconverted friends, walked firmly down the aisle to the altar, and knelt, resolved never to turn back to the world or seek its pleasures while I lived. Others soon followed me for whom I had not looked. We cried aloud, from broken and contrite hearts, fully renouncing every sin; and it was not long before we were all happy in God. I felt that Jesus had taken away the love of the world, and broken the power of every other sin. I knew my heart was changed, for

> " 'Jesus all the day long
> Was my joy and my song.'

"Day after day, during the progress of the revival, a company of us walked to the church several miles often in the mud and rain; but our souls were so blessed that we returned singing the high praises of God.

"So I lived, with the exception of yielding to temptation for a short time once or twice, for a year. At that time I was placed among strangers, attending school with a class of young ladies about me who were strangers to what I had enjoyed. My self-denial, and conscientious course, attracted their observation; and I was pitied, sometimes ridiculed, for my superstitious notions. To avoid their remarks, I said nothing about my religion, and soon began to indulge in the conversation and plays that

were common to all. My teacher was a professed
Methodist, and endeavored to persuade me that my
views were not essential to religion, that I could
dress as others did, and learn the rules of etiquette
necessary to fashionable society without any harm
at all. I tried it so far as I was allowed, and became
impatient of the restraints I had. Still I kept up the
form of religion, was regular at the class and prayer
meeting; but the love of Jesus was killed out of my
soul, and in its place was fostered a love for the
pleasures of the world. Duty becomes irksome.

"I was soon placed in another school, under the
care of a deeply pious lady; and my preceptress
also was one who enjoyed religion. Here, with the
influences thrown about me, I tried to give myself
again to the Lord, and sometimes got within reach
of what I had lost. But I did not obtain it; for as
soon as I again met the sneers of my associates, I
quailed before them, and sank down in silence. My
extremely proud and sensitive nature could not bear
ridicule. The Holy Spirit strove mightily with me;
and on reading Baxter's Saint's Rest, I resolved I
would at least never yield to my proud heart so far
as to give up what form I had, and would seek all
my days for the power. This was a restraint; but
my spirit was restless and unhappy. So I lived on
for three years, striving for deliverance by the deeds

of the law. When I would do good, evil was present with me; and the things I would not, those I did continually. At times I was so fully sensible that I was abiding under the wrath of God that the sudden alarm of danger by accident, or in a thunderstorm, would drive me almost frantic. I would cry for mercy, and promise obedience if my life was spared. But no sooner was all danger over than I found myself harder than ever. Surely, 'His mercy endureth forever.'

"When I was about eighteen, the Holy Spirit once more held me to a decision to walk in the narrow way, that I had always seen was the only way for me. One thing especially was very clear, that if I returned to God, and became all he designed I should be, I must be more completely separate from the world in my dress: I should in this way be committed everywhere as a disciple of Jesus. A certain style of dress was placed before me that I knew had been adopted by a few of my friends who walked with God. It was distinctly shown me that if I would take that path I should have a glorious crown. But it was so revolting to my nature, and the views I had lately tried to cherish, that I answered: No, I never can consent to be so singular as that; others do not see the way so narrow, and if they can be saved so can I. From that time, for

four long years, I could not get so much as a
glimpse again of that which I had always had in
view, though not enjoyed. I grew blinder and darker every hour, and yet more tenacious of my name
and place in the church. Whenever conscience began to reprove me, I hushed its voice with saying:
I am more strict as I am than many who profess
great things, and even enjoy much apparently; and
I shall risk it. Oh, the longsuffering of God! During these four years I indulged more than ever in
my besetting sins, vanity and mirth. And though
my fears and restraints of my profession held me in
check, I loved the circles of pleasure, and took a
transient delight in dress and amusements. My
heart *loved* the world, and had it been suffered by my
parents to follow its bent, would quickly have led
me to destruction. Mistaken friends were not want-
ing who pitied my lot, and upbraided my parents
for their foolish restraints.

"At twenty-two, I was again sent to school for a
year, and, surrounded by those who lived more un-
scrupulously than I was living, my heart and conscience became more and more seared. I was rallied
and entreated to wear *some* ornaments, by my Methodist (?) friends, and soon began to mingle in social
parties. And why not, when they were conducted
and enlivened by my minister, my teachers and my

class-leader? True, there was neither dancing nor
card-playing; but to appear entertaining, we '*must
dress*'*!* A few times I yielded to the prevailing custom; but on one occasion, going home late, too
thinly dressed, from the warm, crowded rooms, I
took a cold that soon settled on my lungs and
threatened a quick consumption. I was guilty before God, and knew his hand was upon me. My
conscience was once more fully roused; and in re-
viewing Butler's Analogy I was so deeply convicted
that I vowed obedience if the Lord would let me
live to get home. The disease was rebuked, and I
was permitted to pass examination and return home
in apparent health. But my vain ambition, so long
fostered, was not easily subdued. When home, I
did set about leading a new life; but every resolve I
made was broken, and the more I asked for light
the darker (as I thought) I grew, till I became so
alarmed at my condition that I told the Lord to
bring me back to himself by any means, lest my
heart should be hardened like Pharaoh's. I promised solemnly, I would now walk in all the light he
gave me. I asked the Lord, if need be, to bring me
down to the gates of death, that I might see myself
in the light of eternity. My prayer was answered,
and in less than three days I was taken suddenly
with what was supposed to be hemorrhage of the

lungs. I was suddenly prostrated, and knew not what hour would be my last. I expected soon to be in eternity; and now I was honest with myself. None but those who have been there can tell how clearly I now saw what it was to be a Christian; how God had been holding, and would hold me responsible for all the light I had enjoyed, or even might have enjoyed, by studying his word in the light of the Holy Spirit. I looked over my life, and could not see where I had been instrumental in the salvation of *one* soul; and while, as a member of the Church militant, my business had been to let my light shine, to labor *continually* for souls, I had not even been saved myself.

"Oh, if I could have obliterated those seven years of idleness in the vineyard, and my example, my influence among my friends—some of whom had gone into eternity without a Saviour, and unwarned by me—I would cheerfully have suffered anything to accomplish it! But these years were gone with their fearful record to the judgment seat; and I had lost the crown I might have had. What a view I had of a starless crown! It seemed to me I could not enjoy heaven if I was permitted to get in barely saved. I wanted an *abundant* entrance. I saw that these seven years I had been living in the church, short of what I knew to be my duty, had been lost;

that during all the time, from the hour I refused to
walk in all the light, I had rested short of salvation;
and that the comforts and blessings I used to have
in the class and prayer meeting, when I would resolve to 'do better,' were only imparted by the heat
around me, and at most were good desires, drawings
of the Father given to lead me to Christ. The Son
of God was not yet revealed in my heart.

"Now that I saw I was a sinner, and had so long
lived one, I cried to God for mercy, for pardon, for
a heart renewed in the image of Jesus. And I obtained it. Glory be to his name! I was led by the
Spirit to a thorough and hearty confession of my
true state, of many things I had done and said to
individuals in my blindness and hardness, to restitu-
tion everywhere, in the smallest matter; and, having
done all *I* could do, then I was once more led to the
blood of Jesus. All weak and helpless, I trusted in
it, and felt its power to save. All my backslidings
were healed.

"And now I began to cry for a clean heart. I saw
I must have this to stand. Pride, impatience, and
the fear of man, must be cast out, or I never could
bear the crosses I saw before me. Here began conflicts I had never dreamed of. Oh, how the Holy
Spirit revealed the native depravity of my heart, in
contrast with the purity needed to make me meet

for the abodes of the blest! I was almost paralyzed
with the views God gave me of the rebellion that
was rooted down deep in my soul. I would have
glorious foretastes of heaven, and constant victory
over my inner foes; but these foes were there, and
I could not, would not rest till they were cast out.
God saw fit to give me such a view of the strength
of the carnal mind as persons do not often have.
As I was in my room one day, alone in prayer, it
seemed for a few moments that the whole strength
of my being rose up, ready to tear God from his
throne rather than to yield to his entire will. I was
shocked at the sight, and so fearful God was about
to leave me to myself that I took hold anew.

"As I was permitted to get out to some meetings
my uncle, Albert G. Terry, was holding, I presented
myself at the altar every evening as a seeker of
holiness. The last night of the week came, and I
was powerfully tempted to abandon the whole thing.
But as I rose to go forward once more, it suddenly
flashed through me, 'If you will go to the front seat
and kneel *there*, facing the whole congregation, and
give up your voice, you will find the help you want.'
I was so desperate, and so glad to see light, that I
obeyed at once; and no sooner had my voice been
surrendered than light and glory broke into my soul.
I was not overpowered, but sank down in silent awe

at the vision of Christ before me, and his streaming
blood pouring through my soul and cleansing even
me. The Spirit said, 'Look where the blood
touches.' I looked, and saw pride washed out, then
anger, revenge, hatred, and so on, clear around my
heart; and then came the clear consciousness that
the work was done. Oh, the sweet heaven of rest!
I did not want to speak or move for some time, lest
I break the spell. My friends seemed disappointed
that I said nothing, and I was fiercely tempted to
think they would not believe me; but God enabled
me to declare all he had done. My faith was in
Jesus' blood. I saw that all my works had not pur-
chased the cleansing; Christ alone had done the
work. I had expected some great demonstrations,
but had not been permitted *one* to lean upon. No
frames or feelings had given me the victory. I had
simply consecrated my voice to God, and it was as
easy then to believe as to breathe.

"I was exhorted by my old class-leader to speak
positively in regard to the work done, whenever
asked, until I knew certainly that I had yielded
to sin; and this advice I followed for years, no matter what were the temptations. There came a time
at length of sore trial, when I was condemned by
those in whom I had always had unbounded confidence; and under the pressure I began to doubt my

real experience, and lost the clear sense of God's cleansing grace. I settled down for awhile into a kind of indifference, from which I seemed to have no power to rally. Many were the conflicts, long and severe, before I was able to get back to the cleansing blood. But Jesus knew my weakness, and did not leave me to the mercy of the enemy. Once more I knew where I stood, independent of all friends or foes."

From this time to her last hour, with, perhaps, the exception of once yielding for a few moments to a sudden temptation, Mrs. La Due enjoyed the experience of perfect love. On all suitable occasions she testified to this fact, and those who were most intimately acquainted with her know that her life did not contradict her profession.

September 19, 1850, she was married to Rev. William Case Kendall; and she shared the toils and triumphs of this able, earnest and spiritual minister until his death, February 1, 1858. An account of his experience and labors, written mostly by herself, and running through eight numbers of the *Earnest Christian*, appeared in the year 1861.

Charges, the utter groundlessness of which may be learned from Terrill's Life of Dr. Redfield and Roberts' Why Another Sect, had been preferred against Mr. Kendall in 1857, and he was to have

been tried at the session of the Genesee conference
of the M. E. church, held at Perry, N. Y., in October, 1858.   But the Lord had taken him away from
the evil to come before this time arrived.   His
widow feared that the conference would not, under
the circumstances, permit a fitting memorial sermon
to be preached; but her fears were not realized, as
the following extract from her journal indicates:

"Tuesday, Oct. 12th—Conference.

"To my great joy, I learn that the letter I
recently wrote to Brother Filmore, in regard to
Brother Roberts preaching the conference funeral
sermon, has probably produced the result of breaking up their plan of refusing any sermon.   A
committee has been appointed, who by Dr. Lucky
have brought before the conference a memoir of
Rev. William C. Kendall, well written, and much
better than I feared they would ever acknowledge.
His usefulness, character, and closing hours, were
justly portrayed.   Dr. Holdich, his old teacher in
the University, arose and gave an honorable account
of his college life.

"I learn all these things were strongly objected
to, and some were impatient at their being suffered;
but the Lord would have his servant honored.

"Brother Roberts, at two o'clock this afternoon,
preached to a full house from, 'I have fought a
good fight, I have finished my course,' etc.   It was
an excellent sermon; and but for the desperate

resistance of his enemies, many of whom sat and ridiculed him, the Spirit would have had free course. As he summed up the history in the conference of my dear companion, the sighs and sobs of the multitude in general rose on every side. The Spirit of the Lord rested upon us in power.

"At the close of the reading of the memoir, the Bishop had given out Wesley's hymn,

"'Come let us join our friends above;'

and it was a solemn, impressive hour. But this afternoon as Brother Abel gave out the tunes, and all joined, it was much more so. Bishop Janes made the closing prayer, and in the simplicity and fervency of the gospel called down upon us the Holy Ghost. I was drawn to him by his holy sympathy, and shall ever remember how he commended me to Jesus, desiring I might take him for my husband. Yes; and I do feel that I have. I have no other arm upon which to lean. He has to-day sustained my soul amidst the idle gaze of hundreds, and the tears also of those multitudes who mourn with me for the early fallen, for the absence of him who drew us all not only to himself, but always nearer to Jesus."

We are here given a glimpse of the opposition to true holiness existing in the Genesee Conference at that time. Further extracts give quite a full view of it, and also show how a few of "God's invincibles" in the face of it all stood steadfastly by the principles of early Methodism.

"Thursday, Oct. 21st, Perry.

"To-day is a day long to be remembered by the pilgrims assembled in the conference room to hear the sentence of Rev. B. T. Roberts. His trial by examining witnesses closed yesterday morning; and in the afternoon he and Brother Stiles summed up the testimony, and made their closing pleas. Brother S. clearly showed that the accused had not been proved a guilty man. He had rather substantiated his innocence. Brother R. spoke in the evening till eight o'clock. God helped him; and a numerous audience were deeply affected by the truths he uttered. The Holy Spirit so pervaded the place that when he closed the opposite counsel was unable to make his rejoinder. It was necessary to wait until this feeling should pass off; and on complaint of an attack of headache the whole was postponed till this morning. He then carried his point, and the votes were to expel."

In June, 1859, Mrs. La Due attended a camp-meeting at Bergen, N. Y., some account of which follows:

"July 3rd—Covington.

"Have just returned, and got rested, from our annual 'feast of tabernacles' at Bergen. Oh, what a refreshing season it has been! How heaven came down to earth!   *   *   *   *

"Dr. Redfield (thank God he was present) let us

have plain, sharp truth, that cut its way, on this point of being valiant for the truth. Many responded heartily; some drew back. Sister H— followed it up, Brother S. K. J. C— coming between to defend God's little ones; and God helped them both, wonderfully, to declare the whole truth.   *   *   *

"On Monday there was a little foretaste of Pentecost. We shall yet have it. As the shower came ou our hearts there was a simultaneous rising all over the ground, with shouts and screams that filled the place with awful glory. We were together from St. Louis, Illinois, Michigan, Oneida, Auburn, Syracuse, Seneca Falls, looking for the baptism of the Holy Ghost. We felt, notwithstanding the conflict, we received a measure of the thing for which we prayed."

In October of this year the Genesee Conference met in annual session at Brockport, N. Y. At the same time a camp-meeting and revival services were conducted near the seat of the conference by Rev. Fay Purdy an evangelist of much power and success. Mrs. La Due gives quite a description of these special meetings, and also refers to the work of the conference, in her journal.

"Tuesday, Oct. 11th—Conference.

"Went into conference this morning, after a sweet

night's rest and a morning ride; but in the crowded
gallery, and amid the turmoil of examining witnesses on Brother Stiles' case, I was weary before
the hour of adjourning and left. I saw a fair sam-
ple of the spirit and designs of the conference 'ma-
jority' toward all who will live godly in Christ Jesus.
But the people know who are worthy of their hire.

"I went on the camp-ground a little while, in the
afternoon; and as I came in sight of the large 'pavil-
ion' surrounded by so many clean, white tents, I
could but think we were near the tents of Israel. I
passed inside the spacious room for public service,
and my soul felt as though all was strangely light
within the tent. Glory filled the place! Brother
A. A. Phelps preached with unusual liberty—his
theme, the responsibility upon the Church, in view
of the immense amount of work to be done in the
ministry, in the Church as a whole, in our church,
in the state and church as to slavery, in the world,
among backsliders and sinners. Oh, what time have
we to be 'at ease in Zion'! Brother Purdy called on
a brother from Wyoming Conference to exhort.
Brother Thurston and others were on the stand.
What a host are here from all parts of the church,
east and through this state, to see 'Nazaritism'!....
Scores came about the altar for salvation. There
were many converted, reclaimed, and sanctified. I

had to leave the sacred spot before evening; but I heard that the sacramental occasion in the night, near twelve o'clock, was a season of thrilling interest. More than six thousand people crowded in and about the tent, and over four hundred came to the altar for communion."

"Wednesday, Oct. 12th.

"Conference has expelled Brother Stiles, after, from Saturday noon till Tuesday night, most exciting and persevering labor. The daily paper has the particulars, and the 'guillotine' plate over it. The people are exasperated beyond endurance. Brothers Cooley, Wells, Burlingham, Reddy, Brooks, Thomas and Farnsworth are under arrest for 'contumacy'—attending irregular meetings held by irregular men; and on Brother Cooley's case they brought out a witness to testify he had clapped his hands on the stand at camp-meeting and said, 'Bless the Lord'!"

In March, 1860, Mrs. La Due went to St. Louis, where she took an active part in revival meetings which Dr. Redfield was conducting in that wicked city.

June 23, 1861, at St. Charles, Illinois, she was united in marriage with Rev. T. S. La Due, to whom she was a most worthy companion until her second bereavement in 1888.

It was doubtless largely owing to her constant attention to Mr. La Due during his last illness that she contracted consumption, the disease of which she died. She was quite low for a time in the winter of 1889. One night she was delirious. One of her sons pleaded in secret with many tears that she might be spared a while longer, if good. It came to him twice, at different times, it would be done. The Lord raised her up that she might, among other things, assist in writing her husband's life before her departure.

She came to Alameda, California, early in January, 1891, on a visit to her younger son. All who saw her at this time remarked that she was failing rapidly. She was not able, after reaching her destination, to attend a single church service. This was a sore trial, as she had always attended the means of grace, if at all possible. But she bore her afflictions with great patience. Notwithstanding her feebleness, her old-time courage was retained, and it was often an inspiration even to be in her presence.

A week or two before her death she took to her bed, and for a time suffered intensely, but was almost entirely free from pain the last two days of her sickness. Satan tempted her powerfully, but she came through into special and glorious victory. A card came from her older son Saturday, April 11. After hearing it read she said, "That's good," and then remarked, "Tell my dear boy John never to doubt his call to preach the gospel. Tell Jennie [his wife] to be sure not to miss the glory of crossing over." A few days before this, when she thought death was at hand, she said, "Tell John this is glorious beyond all description." She left messages for several others, and addressed those about her personally. To her daughter, who had been at her side for some six weeks, she spoke with more than usual earnestness and tenderness.

Sunday night, about 11: 30, she roused up, shouted the praises of God as best she could, and, her face bright with glory, exclaimed, "I'm done with this world forever! I'm done with this *old world* forever!"

About 2:45, Monday morning, April 13, she said to herself twice, "I'm dying forever," evidently meaning, "I'm dying to live forever".

A little later her younger son thought she said, as she looked earnestly toward him, "Sorry."

He enquired, "What are you sorry for, mother?"

But he had not understood her, as he saw when she answered, "*Solid*. I say SOLID." These were her last words—a glorious testimony to die on.

Her son enquired, "Do you mean it's solid under your feet?"

She nodded, yes.

He then asked, "Does the Lord specially bless you yet?" referring to the victory over temptation she had received a day or two before.

She nodded again, yes.

A few moments later, at 3:30 a. m., she passed away so easily that those at her bedside could hardly tell the exact time she ceased breathing.

Brief services were held at the house, Tuesday, at 2 p. m. General Superintendent E. P. Hart spoke a short time from the words, "She hath done what she could." He said she combined in a pre-eminent way the qualities of Mary and Martha,—devotion and service. Quite a number were present.

The body was taken from California to Oregon by steamer, and on April 21 laid beside the remains of Mr. La Due at Gresham. Rev. D. M. Cathey conducted brief services at the grave. Rev. J. C. Scott, who, on account of sickness, was unable to be at the burial, held memorial services at the Sunnyside church, near Clackamas, Oregon, Sunday, May 17.

Mrs. La Due was untiring in her ministrations to the saints, and hundreds will remember her hospitalities at camp meetings and elsewhere. Probably she went too far, at times, in her labors for others;

but certainly this is an uncommon failing in these days. At Owatonna, Minnesota, while yet in middle life, she had an illustrative camp meeting experience. Late at night, after much toil, she got the last one of a large number safely stowed away. She then found there was no place for her; so she sat down, and, leaning her head on some kind of pillow laid on the table, slept until morning. She was glad to do it. She once consecrated herself to wash pots and kettles, if the Lord so pleased. Satan sometimes told her she was fit for nothing else; but she did not take back the consecration.

Her piety was not of an effeminate type, but was characterized by marked fidelity to God, the power of the Holy Ghost, and a grace and unction that increased in richness and strength to the end. Although rather slow, and of a diminutive figure, yet she possessed a faith and persistence that surmounted all difficulties, no matter how high or how long. She was naturally so timid as to suffer intensely when young, even in eating before strangers at her father's table; but her determination, and, above all, the gift of grace gave her a remarkable holy boldness in declaring and defending the truth, either before great congregations or in private. Her words of faithful reproof and rebuke were sometimes sharp as a two-edged sword, causing even those for whom they were not intended to involuntarily hold their breath; but she also possessed a spirit of uncommon tenderness, which endeared her to a host of friends. If she was sometimes too hasty in her judgment, she was always ready to acknowledge her mistake with real humility. She suffered intensely in her own mind whenever she thought her words or actions had been unwise.

She believed the Lord gave her, at different times, several remarkable visions of things unseen and eternal. After Mr. Kendall's death she was at one time overcome with the view which she had of his glorious condition in the heavenly city. In one instance, while praying, she was rebuked and overwhelmed by a sight given her of the condition of a lost soul. She felt this time that she had gone too far, and resolved not to repeat the experiment. As regards the importance and necessity of visions she has said: "If we should never see or hear of what is passing 'behind the veil', the word of God is to be believed as truly as though we saw it all. God does favor us now and then with these illustrations of his word; but they ought not to assume importance above the Scriptures because he thus condescends to our weakness."

Mrs. La Due's plain and neat attire, with her kindly, determined face, gave her the appearance of—

what she was in reality—a Methodist of the old stamp. A good likeness of her, copied from a photograph taken in the spring of 1890, appears opposite the first page of this memoir.

Her home was a hallowed sanctuary, the influence of which can never cease. She leaves three children by her second husband—two sons and one daughter.

The following extract from a letter written by a friend to one of Mrs. La Due's sons, the day after the funeral services at Gresham, Oregon, will be in place here:

"She has gone from us; but she has left an enduring monument, and loving hearts will cherish her sweet memory.

"Before she went up to see you, I heard her say in her testimony, in alluding to the many severe conflicts and trials through which she had passed: 'But I've not had one too many, *not one*. I thank the Lord for them all.' I thought of it yesterday when D— alluded to the persecutions she endured when with Brother Kendall in the M. E. Church, and to the many hardships she and Brother La Due endured; and I think, could she have answered from her home above, we would have heard: 'Not one too many! I've fought a *good* fight.'

"What an example of fidelity, courage, and loving loyalty to God and his cause! As F— G— said to M—, Monday, 'She lived right, and of course she died right.' Fit words, fitly spoken. Right—how she loved the *right*, no matter how unpopular! Regardless of consequences she was its advocate, as 'one of God's invincibles, who can't be killed, and can't be conquered'—as she used so often to say. Truly ours is a great loss."

But for her to die was gain.—

> " Sorrow is solid joy, and pain
>   Is pure delight, endured for thee;
> Reproach and loss are glorious gain,
>   And death is immortality;
> And who for thee their all have given,
>   Have nobly bartered earth for heaven."

As we think of the joys she now shares with that innumerable company who have come "out of great tribulation, and have washed their robes, and made them white in the blood of the Lamb," we can but exclaim, as she did in her last hours on earth, "*O, to be eternally shut in! How glorious!*"

WILLIAM KENDALL LA DUE.

HE following is a brief notice, by General Superintendent Hart, of one who gave much help in the preparation of this book: Rev. William K. La Due died near Soledad, California, at 6:45 a. m., Wednesday, October 31, 1894, aged nearly 30 years.

This short notice chronicles the decease of one of the most remarkable young men I have ever known. A volume would hardly suffice to make known his worth of character and spirit. With a frail physical constitution he inherited mental powers of a high order. Naturally conscientious, and converted when but five years of age, he grew up to be a pure and holy man of God. As a preacher he was far above the average. During the ten years of his labors in the California conference he served nearly every charge, besides being one year chairman of the districts.

351

Well known throughout the bounds of his conference he was universally loved and esteemed. Most pre-eminently he was "The brother whose praise was in all the churches." Not many days before his death, conscious that the end was near, he called his devoted young wife, and on the verge of time, nearing the shores of eternity, calmly dictated the following:

"William Kendall La Due was born at Chili, N. Y., Sunday, February 5, 1865; first found the blessing of the Lord at five years of age; was permanently reclaimed at fourteen at Allentown, Pa.; obtained the blessing of entire sanctification when seventeen, at Highland Park camp meeting, East Oakland, California, in 1882; joined the California conference of the Free Methodist Church in the fall of 1884."

The funeral services were held in the Free Methodist church at San Jose, Rev. F. H. Horton discoursing to a large congregation from 2 Cor. 4: 17, 18; the text having been selected by the deceased just previous to his death.

www.ingramcontent.com/pod-product-compliance
Lightning Source LLC
La Vergne TN
LVHW011216080426
835509LV00005B/154